INTEGRATION WITH MEXICO

ROBERT A. PASTOR

INTEGRATION
WITH MEXICO

OPTIONS FOR
U.S. POLICY

A TWENTIETH CENTURY FUND PAPER

THE TWENTIETH CENTURY FUND PRESS/NEW YORK/1993

The Twentieth Century Fund is a research foundation undertaking timely analyses of economic, political, and social issues. Not-for-profit and nonpartisan, the Fund was founded in 1919 and endowed by Edward A. Filene.

Library of Congress Cataloging-in-Publication Data

Pastor, Robert A.
    Integration with Mexico : options for U.S. policy / by Robert A. Pastor.
        p.   cm.
    "A Twentieth Century Fund paper."
    Includes index.
    ISBN 0-87078-328-9   : $8.95
    1. United States--Foreign economic relations--Mexico.   2. Mexico--Foreign economic relations--United States.   I. Title.
    HF1456.5.M6P37   1993   92-44930
    337.73072--dc20   CIP

Cover Design and Illustration: Claude Goodwin
Manufactured in the United States of America.

FOREWORD

Trade policy brings out the worst in public policy debates: our statistics versus their statistics, academic theories versus economic realities, the interests of companies versus the interests of workers. For while most people usually are better off because of trade liberalization, somebody somewhere gets hurt. Rational discussion, let alone political discourse, is made more difficult because while the benefits of liberalization are abstract and widely scattered, the costs are keenly apparent to those who face the cutting edge of new competition.

These contradictions permeate the discussion of trade issues and are at the heart of our ambivalence over the desirability of trade agreements. Yet the globalization of markets is proceeding rapidly, increasing international competition and driving nations to rethink the rules governing trade. The debate about the North American Free Trade Agreement (NAFTA) is a case in point.

Not surprisingly, NAFTA has been the focus of U.S.-Mexican relations since President Salinas proposed the pact in the spring of 1990. As important as the agreement may be, however, it cannot resolve many issues that are important to future relations between the two countries. Indeed, the closer ties that would accompany the approval of free trade will stimulate an ever-wider set of questions and tensions. American policymakers and the public need to grasp the enduring factors that shape our complex involvement with Mexico, the forces in both countries that underpin a closer union, and the likely consequences of such intimacy, but it will not be an easy discussion.

In the United States, the discussion has been complicated by the fact that although NAFTA was negotiated over the last two years of the

Bush administration, Congress will vote on implementing legislation during the beginning of the Clinton administration. Moreover, the agreement must also be confirmed by the legislatures of the other two nations. The political struggle ahead will not, therefore, be simple. The agreement has provoked a wide range of reactions, ranging from unconditional support to implacable opposition.

If the new partnership of the United States, Mexico, and Canada is to be successful, we will have to think beyond the vexing questions of worker readjustment and environmental impact. These two issues deserve the attention they are getting, but they are only the first of a broad range of topics that properly are part of discussions about what it means to have an open and common market. One need only review the recent experience of the European Community, as well as the long history of our own fifty states, to realize that evolution toward truly free markets requires a constant and continuous reappraisal of a host of existing public policies.

Free trade agreements often are characterized as simple choices between free markets and government intervention. But, in fact, they require more—a new set of government activities. NAFTA should stimulate debate on basic questions about domestic policy, including investment in our work force and the social safety net. The sort of economic integration one sees in Europe, for example, is made politically possible and personally tolerable by the existence of strong social support and worker training on the one hand, and specific economic development commitments to weaker members of the European Community on the other.

This is one of a series of studies the Twentieth Century Fund has undertaken in an effort to contribute to our understanding of the consequences and context of a move toward greater economic integration in North America. This year, the Fund will publish works examining the evolution of hemispheric trade relations beyond NAFTA, U.S. policy toward Cuba, the future of the Organization of American States, and the role of multilateral financial institutions.

Robert Pastor is one of the nation's leading experts on this region. A professor of political science at Emory University and director of the Latin American and Caribbean Program at the Carter Center, Pastor also served on the National Security Council from 1977 to 1981. On behalf of the Trustees, we are grateful for the broad perspective he brings to these difficult and timely issues.

Richard C. Leone, *President*
The Twentieth Century Fund
January 1993

CONTENTS

INTRODUCTION

ON EDGE

From the dawn to the dusk of the twentieth century, Americans* felt assured that it was *their* century, but their confidence had evaporated by 1992. Exit polls on election day, November 3, showed an extremely anxious electorate. The most startling conclusion was that a majority of American voters believed that the nation was not in a cyclical downturn; it was in "a serious long term economic decline."[1] This fear took hold of Americans when the cold war ended, as they began to realize that their country was poorly equipped to compete in a new global economic arena. During the 1980s, the United States had changed from being the world's largest creditor to being its biggest debtor, and wages fell from first to thirteenth among nations. Americans felt their economy was losing ground while Japan and Germany sprinted ahead.[2]

The desire for change and the need to invigorate the U.S. economy were the two main reasons why voters decided to replace an older incumbent with a young leader, Bill Clinton. Voters wanted the new president to concentrate on domestic economic concerns, particularly jobs, and people were increasingly worried that their jobs would be lost

---

* Theoretically, the term "American" should apply to all the people of the Western Hemisphere, but few in Mexico or Latin America would feel comfortable with being called an "American." Therefore, this paper will use the term in its traditional way to apply to a resident of the United States. "North American" will apply to those living in the countries of Canada, the United States, and Mexico.

1

as a result of free trade. The views of America's leaders had long dif-
fered from those of the general public on whether free trade benefited or harmed the U.S. economy, with leaders being very supportive
of free trade. That gap narrowed in the mid-1980s, and by 1990, 83 percent of the American public supported free trade agreements with our
neighbors.

Just two years later, however, as the economy sagged, polls indicated that many more Americans believed that free trade cost jobs than
thought it would help the economy. A substantial majority believed
that the United States should restrict imports to protect jobs and that a
North American Free Trade Agreement (NAFTA) with Mexico and
Canada was a "bad idea."[3] These attitudes were symptomatic of the
nation's fears during a recession. Most economists argued that if translated into policy, these impulses would pull the economy down, just as
a protectionist policy had done in 1930, the first year of the Great
Depression. Yet popular beliefs were too strong and widespread to be
denied or ignored; a new national economic and trade policy would
need to take them into account.

The last years of the twentieth century thus pose a challenge for the
United States: Will it look backward at its finest years, or will it renew
itself? Will it approach problems with a concern solely for domestic
affairs, or will it shape a modern economic strategy that integrates
domestic with international policy?

Ironically, as the United States balanced between turning inward or
forging a new global economic policy, its long-protected, defensive
southern neighbor, Mexico, opted for economic integration with the
United States. Ever since the U.S.-Mexican war in the middle of the
nineteenth century, and particularly since its cataclysmic revolution in
1910, Mexico had tried to insulate itself from the United States and
much of the world. The Mexican government believed that the best
way to defend its sovereignty and develop its economy was to keep the
United States at arms length. It built economic walls of high tariffs and
stringent rules to keep out U.S. goods and investment; it built political
walls around the country and the governing party to control information and prevent the United States from interfering in its politics.

In the 1980s, a severe depression brought on by Mexico's debt crisis
compelled its leaders to rethink their model of economic nationalism
and replace it with an approach that was considered revolutionary, at
least for Mexico. In the spring of 1990, Mexican President Carlos Salinas
de Gortari decided to stop resisting economic integration with the

United States and start promoting it. He proposed to President George Bush that the two governments negotiate a free trade area. For decades, various U.S. leaders had proposed this radical idea to Mexicans, but each previous proposal had met with silence or rejection. Suddenly, the two nations reversed roles. Mexico, the poorer, more conservative country, decided to take a great risk to tie its economic future to the United States, while its richer, stronger neighbor expressed reservations.

In a sense, Canada had initiated the process in 1985 when its prime minister, Brian Mulroney, proposed to then president Ronald Reagan that the two nations negotiate a free trade agreement. This was completed by the end of 1988. In February 1991, Canada joined the U.S.-Mexican negotiations, making them "North American," even though the original agreement with the United States had become very unpopular by this time. Indeed, Canada faced a triple threat: first, Prime Minister Mulroney had become very unpopular; second, most people blamed the trade agreement with the United States for Canada's economic troubles; and finally, on October 26, 1992, Canadian voters rejected a referendum aimed at unifying their divided country. Canada was doubtful about how its parts would relate to each other, let alone how the whole should relate to Washington, D.C., and Mexico City.

The climate for free trade elsewhere was also very uncertain. After thirty-five years, the European Community finally dismantled virtually all of its internal barriers to trade on December 31, 1992, but that triumph marked the end of a year in which the Maastricht Treaty to further "an ever closer union among the peoples of Europe," was rejected in Denmark, delayed in England, and barely supported in France. The people of Europe seemed to be telling their governments that they valued sovereign safeguards more than supranational integration. Meanwhile, the forum for world trade negotiations—the 105-nation General Agreement on Tariffs and Trade (GATT)—perched uncomfortably between completion and the collapse of a six-year effort to lower global barriers to trade. Instead of celebrating the end of the cold war, the nations of the world were distressed about the state of their economies. Without a clear compass or strong leadership, people asked whether insularity or internationalism was a better route to protecting jobs. Many looked to the United States, and the prospect of a new presidency raised hopes and expectations.

The United States has an unprecedented opportunity to tip the balance at home and abroad in favor of a new form of global integration—one that could enhance the environment and benefit not just the multinational corporations but also workers. The first priority for the new president is to rebuild the U.S. economy, but to succeed he cannot separate his domestic from his international agenda, as Franklin D. Roosevelt tried in 1933. He needs to connect his national economic strategy to a new trade policy, and the core of that should be NAFTA.

In a speech on October 4, 1992, presidential candidate Bill Clinton outlined just such an approach. Despite political pressures to oppose the agreement, he pledged to seek its ratification. To try to respond to some of the concerns raised about the pact, he proposed supplemental understandings with Mexico and Canada and implementing legislation that increased adjustment assistance, education, and training for those who would pay the price of free trade by losing their jobs. Two weeks after the election, President Salinas indicated his willingness to negotiate the concerns raised by Clinton.[4]

Given prevailing sentiments in Congress, NAFTA is unlikely to be ratified unless it is modified in this way. A rejection by the United States would probably tip the political balance in Mexico and Canada toward more inward-looking policies, and U.S.-Mexican relations would be set back decades—to the days when more insults were exchanged than goods and services. The Mexican economy could become unsteady if NAFTA is not ratified soon, and the success of Mexico's very complicated political transition may also depend on the agreement. If the United States turns inward, progress in the GATT talks would be adversely affected, and Europe would have still another reason to concentrate its energies on deepening and widening the European Community.

Because the outcome of the debate in all three countries is so uncertain, the agreement has to address the legitimate concerns raised by many of its critics. In each of the three countries, there are fears of being overrun or undermined by a neighbor, and it is unfair and unwise to pretend that the fears have no basis. But there are also hopes of prosperity through integration; these hopes can only prevail if policies are devised to minimize the prospect that the fears come true, or that the agreement could be reversed.

Canada joined NAFTA to ensure that its interests are preserved from the Canadian-U.S. Free Trade Agreement, which was more important to Canadians. Less than 2 percent of the trade of Canada and Mexico is with the other, though this two-way trade is growing, whereas more than two-thirds of the trade of each is with the United States. So NAFTA is primarily a U.S.-Mexican agreement. Its scope is making it the centerpiece of the bilateral relationship. NAFTA provides an opportunity for the two countries to overcome the burden of a troubled history and find a common language. But it also contains the seeds of possible future conflicts.

The trade negotiators tried to keep the focus on issues of trade and investment, but the U.S. Congress, reflecting public opinion, has insisted on a broader social, economic, and political agenda. When the formal debate on the agreement begins, one can expect concerns about human rights and other practices to be pressed upon Mexico. A senator, for example, might insist that a particular element of the agreement should be implemented only if Mexico respects the vote, or if it stops selling its oil at below-market prices to its petrochemical industry. The signing of the agreement on December 17, 1992, therefore did not signify the end of negotiations, but rather the beginning of a continual process of managed economic integration.

NAFTA's importance extends beyond its effect on U.S.-Mexican relations. With modifications, a new NAFTA could contribute to reactivating the U.S. economy, making our companies more competitive, and shoring up American leadership in the world. The new president has a chance to assemble a new coalition of interests behind an innovative trade program, which would extend NAFTA to the entire hemisphere and permit the United States to reshape the international trading system.

The purpose of this study is to examine the options available to the United States and its neighbors to enhance integration in NAFTA and beyond. "Integration" does not imply that the borders will blur and a single North American state will emerge soon. Decades from now, such an idea may not be inconceivable, but today it would be so repugnant to many leaders in Mexico and Canada and so alien to Americans that its mere mention could sow discord. Economic integration means that trade and investment among the three countries will grow faster than their combined gross national product. Social integration means that contact and immigration among the peoples of the three countries will expand more rapidly than interactions with other countries. And political integration means that there will be more involvement by each in the politics and policies of the others than ever before. That has already begun. The Mexican government, always the most reticent of the three, has dramatically expanded its lobbying and public relations activities in Washington and throughout the United States. This is a positive development; the more that each country engages the other, the better.

As groups within Mexico reach out to try to influence the debate in the United States, new transnational and transgovernmental alliances will take shape, changing the way that people and governments of the North American countries relate to one another. U.S. and Canadian labor unions will link arms with Mexican intellectuals to stress the agreement's flaws, while businessmen in all three countries will put its best face forward.

A new era of friendliness and cooperation will not necessarily follow the increasing economic, social, and political integration. Actually, as each country becomes more dependent on the other, new tensions will be unavoidable. Old problems will resurface. The experiences of the European Community demonstrate that integration does not move forward in a straight line; it stalls, or changes direction, and reversals are always possible. To cope with the increasing exchanges and to make sure that the trilateral debate remains constructive, new institutions and procedures will be needed. Otherwise, NAFTA will lead to less cooperation, not more.

Chapter 1 describes the history that shaped the current relationship between Mexico and the United States and examines the interests that the United States has in the development of its southern neighbor.

Chapter 2 explains the political and psychological parameters within which each country debates integration. All parties are of at least two minds about closer relations, and an offensive remark by one side can strengthen the opponents of integration in another country. This debate intersects with the normally fractious politics of trade, making integration even more precarious.

Chapter 3 describes the agreement and estimates its impact on the three economies of North America and on different groups. The conclusion is that all three countries will benefit, but Mexico will benefit the most and Canada the least, and certain sectors will pay a price in each country.

In Chapter 4, there is an evaluation of the new issues of interdependence that have challenged NAFTA: the environment, social issues, and human rights.

Chapter 5 summarizes Bill Clinton's proposal on NAFTA and, using that as an outline, offers some ideas on how to use the strengths of a freer market to produce and allocate goods and services while compensating for the market's weaknesses or dysfunctions. In addition, the negotiating partners need to anticipate tensions, seek new opportunities, and learn lessons from Europe's experience. Finally, the chapter suggests some ways that the U.S. government should be reorganized to ensure that NAFTA is integrated with its domestic and geopolitical policies.

Chapter 6 reviews the hemispheric and global implications of NAFTA with an eye to understanding how the agreement will relate to and affect the world. NAFTA has great potential to be extended to a hemispheric free trade area and to offer formulas and serve as a model for the global trading system.

* * *

Between the election and his inauguration, while he selected a cabinet and developed his budget and economic policies, Bill Clinton could not avoid the multiple global crises from Somalia to Bosnia, Iraq, and Haiti. Leaders, including British Prime Minister John Major and Russian President Boris Yeltsin, sought personal meetings, but to underscore the priority he attached to domestic concerns, he declined all of them—except for Mexican President Carlos Salinas. In addition, Clinton announced that Canadian Prime Minister Brian Mulroney would be his first state visitor after the inauguration. North America, correctly, came first.

During his meeting with Salinas in Texas on January 8, President-elect Clinton pledged to move promptly to negotiate the outstanding labor and environmental issues so that "we can move forward in building a strong relationship between our two countries and in concluding a successful trade negotiation." He also described NAFTA as the "foundation for further trade agreements" with the rest of the Americas. The gesture to his neighbors and the comments were encouraging steps on the road to a new North American trading entity, a refashioned hemisphere, and an invigorated world trading system.

CHAPTER 1

MEXICAN WALLS AND AMERICAN INTERESTS

Former Secretary of State James A. Baker III said that "the United States does not have any relationship more important than the one it has with Mexico."[1] Nor is any more frustrating, difficult, and complex. Mexicans can explain the symptoms best. In 1979, then President José López Portillo described the "recurring vague fears" that North Americans "inspire in certain areas of our national consciousness."[2] Unlike López Portillo, who appeared to prefer a cool relationship with the United States, Carlos Salinas de Gortari, who took office in December 1988, deliberately chose a more cooperative approach. Instead of interpreting every perceived slight from the United States as a threat to Mexico's sovereignty, as many of his predecessors had done, Salinas and his administration did the opposite, downplaying discord and trying to resolve serious problems. But even Salinas, the pragmatist, acknowledged: "Relations with such a powerful neighbor, with the most complex common border in the world and a history burdened by acts of extreme aggression, will never be easy."[3]

THE BEST DEFENSE

It is not hard to locate the origins of the troubled relationship. For Mexico, the loss of more than one-third of its territory to the United States in the middle of the nineteenth century; a nineteen-hundred-mile border with a superpower; the long historical resentment of being overtaken by a country that its elite viewed as unrefined; the fear of being overwhelmed by the U.S. economy and its consumer culture—all these have led Mexico to build economic, political, and legal walls to keep the United States from interfering with or even influencing its internal affairs. Any intrusion has met with a stalwart reaction; even the opening of a McDonald's restaurant in downtown Mexico City evoked violent strikes and fears that Mexico's culture might be endangered by American cheeseburgers.

Faced with such a fearsome, pushy neighbor, Mexico has used its guile to define the limits to the relationship by "just saying no," sometimes quietly, other times defiantly. "We will neither be run over nor erased from the map," warned President López Portillo,[4] as if the United States considered these to be options. Mexico devised a plethora of tactics to put Washington on the defensive by claiming that it was trying to put Mexico on the defensive.

The walls, of course, served other purposes. Tariff walls protected Mexican businessmen from economic competition, but the country's closed system also permitted consistent economic growth, averaging 6 percent per year, from 1940 to 1982. The instruments of political control shielded the governing Institutional Revolutionary Party (PRI) from criticism or defeat and kept the poor, darker-skinned masses from threatening the privileged strata of society, but they also provided a high degree of political stability in a region wracked by military coups.

The job of Mexico's diplomats was to man the ramparts and warn their countrymen and the world of the earliest sign that Washington would interfere in Mexico's internal affairs. U.S. government officials found such charges and the attitude that produced them baffling, and attributed it to the fact that "Mexico has tended . . . to define [its] foreign policy in opposition to ours."[5] But over time, the United States learned to respect Mexico's differences and its need for some distance.

Some Mexicans, like Jorge G. Castañeda, candidly acknowledged that a Mexican foreign policy that is "contrary to American interests, constitutes a sort of shield for Mexico. Only behind such a shield can the country proceed successfully with the delicate and exceedingly difficult balancing act it must carry out—opening its windows to the world without forsaking its national integrity. . . ."[6]

U.S. INTERESTS

Why should the United States bother? Aside from those living near the border and those responsible for managing the relationship in Washington, most Americans do not pay much attention to Mexico. They should for several reasons.

First, Mexico is a country of growing weight and importance to the United States. Its border is the longest separating a developing from an industrialized country. With 83 million people in 1991, Mexico is the eleventh most populous nation in the world, with the thirteenth-biggest economy and land area. It has extensive natural resources; its reserves of oil, gas, silver, lead, and copper rank among the top six countries in the world. It also has a growing middle class, symbolized by the fact that only seven countries have more automobiles than Mexico.[7]

The most staggering traffic, however, has not been within Mexico but between it and the United States. In 1990 alone, there were more than 270 million legal border crossings from Mexico into the United States, an average of about three-quarters of a million people each day.[8]

Of course, the daily movement of people between the two countries affects them less than the number who remain and settle north of the border. Since the northern part of Mexico was incorporated into the United States in the nineteenth century, Mexicans have been an important ethnic group, but immigration from Mexico was quite small for most of U.S. history. During the congressional debate on immigration quotas in 1921, little thought was given to restricting immigrants from Mexico because, as Senator Alva Adams of Colorado said, "Remember, Mexico is not a populous country."[9] That, of course, changed after the Second World War, as Mexico's population mushroomed from 26 million in 1950 to 67 million in 1980. In the past three decades (1960–1990), the United States received 15.1 million immigrants from more than one hundred nations. Nearly one in every five (2.75 million, or 18.1 percent) came from Mexico. Recent Mexican legal immigration has occurred at a substantially higher rate than that from the United Kingdom in the nineteenth century or from the Philippines (the second-largest source today at 4.6 percent of all legal immigrants). Of the foreign-born population in the United States, 21.7 percent are from Mexico.[10] Most of those have come recently; 71 percent of all Mexican legal immigrants to the United States arrived during the past three decades. (See Table 1.1, page 12.)

Not all Mexicans have come legally. In the 1980s, apprehensions of undocumented workers averaged about 1 million each year, with 1.2 million in 1990. More than 90 percent of these workers have been from Mexico.[11] Altogether, more than three times as many legal and illegal migrants have come to the United States from Mexico as from any other country.[12] According to surveys of Mexicans by the *New York Times* and the *Los Angeles Times*, 38 to 50 percent of Mexicans have indicated that

TABLE 1.1
IMMIGRATION TO THE UNITED STATES
1820–1990

	All Countries	Mexico	Mexico as % of All	United Kingdom	Philippines
1820–1860	5,062,414	17,766	0.35	794,317	na
1861–1900	14,061,192	10,237	0.07	1,626,938	na
1901–1920	14,532,297	268,646	1.85	867,358	na
1921–1930	4,107,209	459,287	11.18	339,570	na
1931–1940	528,431	22,319	4.22	31,572	528
1941–1950	1,035,039	60,589	5.85	139,306	4,691
1951–1960	2,515,479	299,811	11.92	202,824	19,307
1961–1970	3,321,677	453,937	13.66	213,822	98,376
1971–1980	4,493,314	640,294	14.25	137,374	354,987
1981–1990	7,338,062	1,655,843	22.56	159,173	548,764
		Total			
1820–1990	56,994,014	3,888,729	6.82	5,119,150	1,026,653

Source: U.S. Department of Justice, Immigration and Naturalization Service, *Statistical Yearbook, 1990* (Washington, D.C.: Government Printing Office, 1991).

they have a close relative living in the United States. This suggests that the statistics might understate substantially the real presence of Mexicans.

Mexicans are reshaping the societies of the fast-growing states of California and Texas and, more broadly, of the entire United States. The 1990 census showed that the country's racial mix was altered "more dramatically in the past decade than at any time in the 20th century," with the minority population rising from 20 to 25 percent of the total. In fact, the rate of increase of the minority population was twice as fast as in the 1970s. Half of the increase in the total number of Hispanics—from 14.6 to 22.4 million—was due to immigration. About two-thirds of the Hispanics were from Mexico, and more than half of the Mexicans live in California and Texas.[13]

The United States has a sovereign interest in defending its southern border, but that task has proven more complicated over time. Geographically, the connection between the two contiguous regions— the southwestern part of the United States and the northern part of

Mexico—has become so intimate as to begin to constitute, in some minds, a third nation.[14] This new border reality, like many other characteristics of the relationship, arouses pride and fear in different groups. The population on the border is quite small compared with the total population of the two countries, but it has been growing at a much faster rate than that of either country. In Mexico, the fastest-growing cities are on the border; between 1950 and 1980, the population living near the border increased 355 percent, with three previously small towns (Tijuana, Ciudad Juárez, and Mexicali) now ranking among Mexico's ten largest cities.[15]

The northern part of Mexico has always looked at itself and at the United States differently than the central region, which includes Mexico City and the traditional centers of civilization. The northern states' economies are the most modern; their contacts with the United States are the most straightforward. It is not a coincidence that Carlos Salinas comes from the north.

At the same time that Mexicans were moving north, to the border and sometimes beyond, Americans were moving south toward the "Sunbelt." Just between 1980 and 1986, the Sunbelt's population increased at ten times the rate of that of the Northeast and Midwest.[16] The region's population expanded because of migration from both the north and south, and because of a higher fertility rate for Mexican-Americans. The result was an increasing homogenization on both sides of the border. In Los Angeles, which contains the second-largest school district in the United States, the ratio of Anglo to Mexican-American students reversed in just two decades; from 56 percent Anglo and 19 percent Hispanic (almost all Mexican-Americans) in 1966 to 18 percent Anglo and 56 percent Hispanic in 1986.[17] (Contributing to this trend was the exodus of whites from the public school system.)

Although U.S. trade with Mexico originates in forty-five states, the bulk comes from those closest, particularly Texas and California. In 1990, these two states accounted for $18 billion in exports to Mexico, more than 60 percent of the U.S. total.[18]

The most vigorous example of the growing integration of the two economies has been the "maquiladoras"—production-sharing plants built on the Mexican side of the border to exploit the comparative advantage of both countries. Since the mid-1960s, companies owned mostly by Americans have imported components from the United States to be assembled by cheap Mexican labor. A U.S. tariff provision permits the manufacturer to pay duty only on the "value-added" part of the product—that is, the value of the labor and the Mexican materials added to the product.

Peso devaluations in the 1980s widened the wage disparity between Mexican and U.S. labor, stimulating an industrial takeoff along the border. By December 1990 there were 2,000 maquiladoras employing 500,000 workers, about 20 percent of Mexico's total manufacturing work force. Maquiladoras doubled their exports to the United States from $5.6 billion, or 29 percent of total Mexican exports, in 1985 to $11.9 billion, or 45 percent, in 1989.[19]

Mexico's increasing weight in U.S. calculations owes not just to the population explosion, the immigration wave, or growth along the border. Beginning in the early 1970s, vast new discoveries of oil transformed Mexico from a net importer into a major exporter, and it became the largest supplier of the U.S. strategic petroleum reserve. Oil exports permitted Mexico to buy more from the United States in the 1980s, lifting it to the status of the third-largest U.S. trading partner—behind Canada and Japan, but ahead of Britain and Germany. From 1971 to 1981, U.S. exports to Mexico increased ten times, from $1.78 billion to $17.78 billion, and then nearly doubled again, to $33.3 billion in 1991 (see Figure 1.1). During this period, the importance of trade with Mexico as a percentage of total U.S. trade nearly doubled. U.S. exports continue to soar. From January through September 1992, U.S. exports to Mexico increased 26.1 percent above the corresponding figure for 1991.[20]

Even more impressive than the rising volume of trade was the change in the composition of Mexican exports to the United States. Oil constituted 80 percent of Mexico's exports across the border in 1982, but just 32 percent in 1991; concurrently, manufacturing exports increased from 14.2 percent to 59.2 percent.[21] If under-the-counter, unregistered transactions were included (and certainly if the illegal drug trade were added), Mexico might be the largest trading partner of the United States.

Although direct investment was restricted by Mexican law, U.S. interests owned about 50 to 65 percent of all foreign direct investment in Mexico during the 1980s. But the total amount of U.S. investment tripled from $7.6 billion in 1983 to $21.5 billion in 1991.[22] There were no restrictions on lending money, however, and Mexico borrowed billions of dollars from American banks in the 1970s. When the Mexican finance minister announced in August 1982 that his government could not service the debt, seven of the nine largest U.S. banks faced the prospect of bankruptcy as a result, shaking the banking system to its

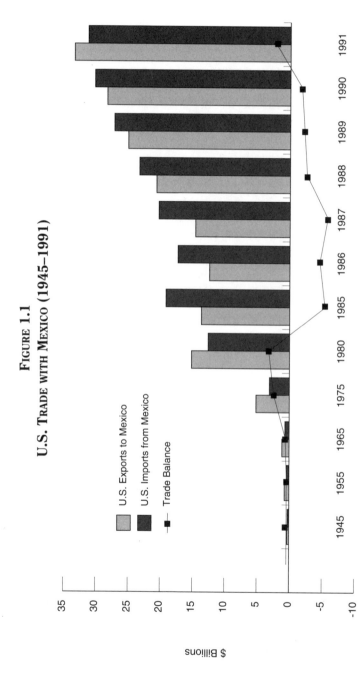

FIGURE 1.1
U.S. TRADE WITH MEXICO (1945–1991)

Source: U.S. Department of the Census, Bureau of the Census, *Statistical/Abstract of the United States*, various issues, 1950–1991 (Washington, D.C.: Government Printing Office).

core. The Reagan administration discarded its laissez-faire ideology in favor of helping Mexico pay the debt; it could no longer ignore the economic consequences for the United States of increasing economic interdependence with Mexico.

With the collapse of the Soviet Union, there is probably no country in the world that can have as much of an impact on the national security of the United States as Mexico. In thinking about U.S. relations with Mexico, the very concept of "national security" needs to be expanded and refined. U.S. concern with Mexico does not stem from any balance of armaments or military power, nor does Mexico pose a threat, as conventionally understood, to the United States. But the consequences of economic depression in Mexico are felt immediately in the United States. In order to pay its foreign debt, Mexico had to rein in its imports, and as a result, from 1981 to 1983, U.S. exports to Mexico fell by about half, from $18 to $9 billion. With each billion dollars of exports accounting for about 20,000 U.S. jobs, Mexico's debt crisis was rapidly passed on to the United States in the form of deepening unemployment. Moreover, the downturn also meant more undocumented workers fleeing northward, with apprehensions on the border doubling in four years, to a peak of 1,767,400 in 1986.[23]

The effect on the United States of Mexico's economic deterioration in the 1980s is insignificant compared to what would happen if there were serious instability in Mexico. Given the ties that connect families in the two countries, instability would provoke a flight of both capital and people on a massive scale. American citizens resident in Mexico would no doubt be caught in the violence, and their property would be affected. The U.S. president would be pressured to act, just as William Howard Taft was during the Mexican revolution in 1910. A moment of internal crisis would no doubt cause the Mexican government to feel embattled and even more resistant to U.S. influence than ever. Thus, there might be little that the United States could do effectively to end the instability or assist in recovery at that time, while there is much the United States might do that could exacerbate Mexico's problems by provoking a nationalistic reaction.

Mexico's importance to the United States, in brief, stems from four sets of interests. Each has both a positive and negative dimension. First, the United States is fortunate to have a secure, nonfortified border but is unable to shield itself from the consequences of adverse developments, whether economic, political, or security-related, in Mexico. Second, as a result of the enormous wave of cross-boundary migration over the last three decades, social integration is relatively well-advanced, and a growing community has an important stake in the two countries. This enriches both cultures and eases communication. Our neighbors to the south no longer look so foreign or distant to us, nor we to them. Moreover, the new Mexican residents have exhibited a strong desire for assimilation; 90 percent of them agree that immigrants should learn English.[24] Notwithstanding, immigration makes some Americans anxious that their "American identity" could be diluted, and the ideas that flow with the people have made it more difficult for the Mexican government to control information.

Third, the border community has become a thermometer of the relationship. In 1969, and again in 1985, the U.S. government deliberately slowed traffic on the border to protest Mexico's lack of cooperation on drug-related issues, and Mexico's fever shot up. Both countries have a stake in managing the border's special problems in a respectful way that keeps the temperature normal and improves the overall relationship. Fourth, the economies are increasingly interconnected; that is unfortunate when there is a problem like the debt crisis, but it also presents great opportunities for trade and investment.

A Breach in the Walls and Down They Come

When Mexico's state-controlled economic model failed in the early 1980s, some leaders in the PRI realized that the time had come to develop a new model. President Miguel de la Madrid began to change the direction of Mexico's economic policy, from a closed system based on import-substitution industrialization to one that was more export-oriented. Mexico joined GATT in 1986 and the next year negotiated a "framework" agreement with the United States to consult on lowering trade and investment barriers between the two countries. He also began to deregulate the economy. But de la Madrid was a cautious man. He realized that many in his party opposed his changes. He slowed the reforms, but it was too late to prevent a significant political breach in the previously impregnable PRI. Cuauhtémoc Cárdenas, the son of a very popular Mexican president who had nationalized the oil industry, left the party and challenged Carlos Salinas for the presidency and for the PRI's soul and legacy. To his credit, de la Madrid broke with past practice and tolerated the dissident movement. During the 1988 election campaign, the candidates offered different answers to the question of how to escape the economic crisis. Salinas promised to continue the economic opening and negotiate debt relief. Cárdenas called for a moratorium on debt payments and promised to return to the old PRI traditions. Salinas was declared the victor with a bare majority in a seriously disputed election, but Cárdenas charged fraud and refused to accept the results.

The economy continued to decline during the transition period following the election, and there were rumors of a possible coup. Salinas took office on December 1, 1988, and in his first hundred days, he moved swiftly and with authority. He sent the army to arrest the corrupt union boss of PEMEX, who had turned Mexico's state oil company from the nation's golden egg into its white elephant. Then he moved with equal vigor to arrest businessmen for illegal trading or for not paying taxes, well-known drug traffickers who had controlled local or state governments, and even a senior government official on the charge of murdering a famous journalist.

Salinas's economic priority was to reduce his country's external debt. He assembled a brilliant economic team and persuaded President Bush and Secretary of the Treasury Nicholas Brady to modify the U.S. policy to permit debt reductions; Mexico became the first country to negotiate debt relief under the Brady Plan. The agreement was completed in late July 1989 and signed on February 4, 1990, with the Bank Advisory Committee, representing roughly five hundred commercial banks with loans to Mexico. As a result of that agreement, Mexico's external debt was reduced from about $100 billion in 1988 to an equivalent of around $85.8 billion in 1990. More significant, Mexico would save about $4 billion in debt service each year from 1990 to 1994.[25] The ratio of gross external debt to GDP declined by half, to 36.8 percent, in 1991; interest payments in 1990 sank to 20 percent of the value of exports, less than half of the proportion paid during the height of the debt crisis.[26]

Salinas raised revenues 13.4 percent by enforcing the tax laws for the first time in Mexican history, and he cut public expenditures. The fiscal deficit shrank from 11.7 percent of GDP in 1988 to 5.8 percent the next year, and the government produced a budgetary surplus in 1992. Inflation plummeted from 160 percent in 1987 to 19.7 percent in 1989, and then to 10 percent in 1992. The number of state enterprises fell from 1,155 in 1982 to 412 in 1988 to 232 in 1992.[27] Deregulation permitted businesses to respond to market signals rather than to bureaucrats.

Trade barriers were lowered so sharply that Mexico went from being one of the most protected markets in the world—with import licenses on virtually every product and a maximum tariff of 100 percent—to one of the most open, with an average weighted tariff of 9.5 percent. Manufacturing exports surged.[28] After fleeing north for a decade, capital began to return to Mexico. The nation's stock of foreign direct investment doubled from $17.1 billion in 1986 to $34 billion in 1991,[29] nearly reaching Salinas's five-year goal two years ahead of schedule.[30] In 1991 alone, Mexico received $12.3 billion in foreign investment flows, composed of $4.8 billion of direct investment and $7.5 billion of portfolio investment.[31]

Salinas not only changed policies; he also tried to change the way Mexicans thought about the role of the state. In his first state of the nation report on November 1, 1989, he criticized the "outmoded view that confuses being progressive with being statist. . . . In Mexico, a larger state has resulted in less capacity to respond to social demands."[32] He then revised the rules on foreign investment to permit foreign ownership of Mexican firms, and he even relaxed some restrictions on foreign investment in mining and agriculture, despite firm postrevolutionary opposition to foreign ownership in these sectors.[33] Finally, he privatized Mexico's eighteen largest banks, which had been nationalized in 1982 under López Portillo.

In 1989, at the outset, there was little or no confidence in the economy, and many questioned Salinas's commitment to a free market. By the summer of 1990, no one questioned Salinas's commitment, and confidence was returning. The rate of economic growth was 3.3 percent in 1989, 4.4 percent in 1990, and 3.6 percent in 1991—the first real improvement since the onset of the debt crisis.[34] The oil price increase that came as a result of the war in the Persian Gulf provided an additional windfall, but, this time, Mexico's new pragmatists were determined to avoid their predecessors' mistake of treating the oil boom as permanent. The government not only refrained from spending the extra $3 billion, it sheltered the windfall in a separate account to compensate for the possibility of a future slide in prices, which, in fact, occurred the next year.[35]

Within two years of Salinas's inauguration, the new Mexican economic strategy was in place and working. "The country that started Latin America's debt crisis in 1982," wrote *The Economist*, "is leading a trinity of reformed debtors—including Venezuela and Chile—back to international markets a decade later."[36] Salinas's economic strategy was not unique. The basic elements represented a new Latin-American consensus on the most effective path to development. What was special about Mexico was Salinas's decisiveness and the economy's quick response. Ironically, the one element of the new Mexican strategy that would have the greatest influence on Latin America was not even a part of the original strategy—the proposal for a free trade agreement with the United States.

Americans had proposed a free trade agreement with Mexico on previous occasions, never to any enthusiasm on the Mexican side. Even Salinas had argued against such an arrangement because of the disparities between the two economies.[37] In the spring of 1990, however, he changed his mind. Why?

"Two elements. First, we opened the economy to reduce inflation," Salinas responded in an interview. Since Mexico no longer protected its market, its challenge was to secure access to the U.S. market. "Secondly, the changes in Europe and East Asia and an apparent reliance on blocs convinced me that we should also try to be part of an economic trading bloc with the United States and Canada. But," he insisted, "we do not want this bloc to be a fortress. We want it to strengthen our ability to be part of Asia, Europe, and especially Latin America."[38]

Salinas needed new investments to move his economy forward, but he found Western Europe preoccupied by the end of the cold war and by the deepening of the European Community, and he perceived that Japan was focused on Asia and hesitant about taking the initiative in an area the United States viewed as a vital interest. The traditional Mexican strategy had been to try to gain U.S. attention by making feints toward other regions, but Salinas reversed direction. *After* proposing a free trade agreement with Washington, he traveled to Japan, where he converted incipient Japanese interest in using Mexico's guaranteed access to the U.S. market into $2 billion worth of commitments for new investments—equivalent to the level of Japanese investment in Mexico at that time.

AMERICAN AMBIVALENCE

In one of the ironic role reversals that characterizes the U.S.-Mexican relationship, George Bush responded cautiously to the Salinas proposal. He suggested waiting until after the multilateral "Uruguay Round" GATT trade negotiations were completed, which he expected to be achieved by December 1990. Bush was later persuaded by friends and lobbyists to move more rapidly,[39] and on September 25, 1990, he notified Congress of his intent to negotiate a free trade agreement with Mexico.

Bush's uncertain reaction anticipated congressional resistance to the idea and was symptomatic of the declining confidence of the United States in its economic status in the post-cold-war world. The United States had maintained a trade surplus from the end of World War II until 1971. During the 1970s, however, the nation ran constant annual trade deficits that only worsened in the 1980s. From 1980 to the summer of 1992, the U.S. government quadrupled its debt, to more than $4 trillion. Interest payments on the debt rose 50 percent, accounting for about 15 percent of the federal budget.[40]

By the 1990s, it was clear that the hemorrhaging budget deficit crippled domestic savings and investment, reduced present and future growth rates, hampered competitiveness, and made the country more vulnerable to the vagaries of foreign capital. At the same time, U.S. economic policies exacerbated domestic income inequalities, transferred resources from savings to consumption, and from infrastructure and education to defense and entitlements. During the 1980s, the richest 1 percent of the American people paid 30 percent less in taxes than they had before Reagan's tax acts, but they earned 60 percent of the growth in the nation's after-tax income.[41] The gap between the rich and poor widened, and the middle class shrank.[42] The riots in Los Angeles in 1992 were a manifestation of a deep-seated social crisis that had been ignored too long.

The United States no longer had the capital generated by the steady trade surplus to lead as it had done in the late 1940s, and that may be one of the reasons for the lack of progress in GATT negotiations. Ideologically, U.S. leaders were still committed to a global trading system and resistant to trading blocs, but, within the United States, demands grew for protecting jobs. In this light, Bush's ambivalent reaction reflected the uncertainty of the nation.

Still, few groups in the United States paid much attention to trade issues with Mexico until Bush asked Congress for "fast-track negotiating authority" for NAFTA. Many in Congress articulated the concerns raised by different groups. American labor worried about lost jobs or reduced wages. The American public was tiring of the large influx of immigrants and wanted it stopped; more than two-thirds of the American public said that there were already too many Latin-American immigrants.[43] Environmentalists were concerned that U.S. companies might relocate to avoid U.S. environmental laws. Others were troubled about the authoritarianism of Mexico's politics, or fearful that the differences in wealth and political and legal systems in the two countries might make such an agreement unworkable.

On May 1, 1991, President Bush sent a letter with a detailed action plan to Democratic leaders in Congress, assuring them that their concerns would be addressed in the NAFTA negotiations. After an arduous debate, the House of Representatives on May 23 squelched a resolution of disapproval by a vote of 231 to 192. The next day, the Senate did the same, 59 to 36. At the same time, both houses approved a resolution stating that fast-track authority was granted only because Congress expected the president to accomplish the objectives that he described in his May 1 letter. With the transfer of negotiating authority, the unofficial talks, which had been conducted for almost a year, became formal negotiations in June.

Although the negotiators predicted an agreement could be completed in early 1992, the talks continued until the summer for a number of reasons. Although many had initially thought that NAFTA would merely expand the U.S.-Canadian agreement, this proved impossible because of the wide differences in political cultures, legal frameworks, and levels of development between the two industrialized countries and Mexico. Carla Hills, the U.S. negotiator, was tough and practical-minded, and she attached less importance to NAFTA than to GATT. She also believed that the only way either agreement would be ratified was by responding fully to the private sector's demands. She therefore pressed the Mexicans for access to their energy resources, financial institutions, and agriculture on behalf of U.S. companies. Although the Mexican negotiators were anxious for an agreement, they could concede little in these politically sensitive areas.

Negotiations thus dragged on much longer than either side had expected. Finally, at a summit meeting in San Diego on July 14, 1992, both Presidents Salinas and Bush compared their political agendas. Bush wanted to complete an agreement before the Republican National Convention in Houston the next month, and Salinas wanted it initialed before the Mexican state of the nation report (*informe*) on November 1, 1992. Both understood that ratification would have to await the seating of a newly elected U.S. Congress, but they gave clear instructions to their negotiators to reach agreement in early August and have the texts ready for initialing before Salinas's *informe* and the U.S. presidential election. Those instructions were followed.

CHAPTER 2

THE TWIN LOGICS OF THE DEBATE:
INTERACTING FEARS AND HOPES

The North American free trade negotiations were conducted by three very pragmatic teams of technocrats. Their job was to decide how much and how fast to lower North American trade and investment barriers. Within each of the three countries, however, the debate covered a far more extensive agenda, including political issues like human rights violations and cultural questions such as the preservation of national identity. Each team's position was shaped by the ratification process and by political concerns.

Mexico's president has constitutional and political powers that would make his northern compatriots swoon. Furthermore, Salinas's party controls sixty-one of sixty-four seats in the Senate, although only a majority is needed to approve the treaty. The easy approval of the agreement, however, should not lead one to overlook the subtle and subterranean debate on NAFTA in Mexico. Of the opponents of NAFTA in all three countries, Mexico's seem to have the least influence, but in the long term, they may have the greatest power to reverse the agreement because of the historical and lingering anxiety about the dangers of getting too close to the United States.

In Canada, Prime Minister Brian Mulroney is very unpopular, and the entire governing system is under severe strain. Nonetheless, Canadian ratification should theoretically be easy, in the context of the country's parliamentary system, particularly because NAFTA is not an important agreement for Canada given its limited trade with Mexico. On the other hand, after the defeat of the October 1992 constitutional referendum, and with the continuing decline of the economy, Mulroney might lose an election that he must call before the fall of 1993. If so, NAFTA could be discarded by the new government. (NAFTA has a clause allowing each government to withdraw after six months.)

The U.S. Congress is by far the most independent of the three legislatures. With the signing of NAFTA having taken place on December 17, 1992, the implementing legislation can be introduced in Congress whenever it is ready and President Clinton and congressional leaders feel the moment is right. Clinton said that he wants three side agreements to accompany the legislation. It is not clear how much of a delay that will cause. Although fast-track negotiating authority expires on May 31—and requires a request by March 2 for an extension—he may not need that authority to negotiate the side agreements that he outlined. These can take the form of executive agreements or understandings. The implementing legislation will be written by the staff of the Senate Finance and House Ways and Means committees and the trade negotiators, so the congressional leaders have a stake in getting it approved.[1] Because the congressional debate is so open, groups from all three countries will use the leverage provided by the congressional forum to advance their agendas. The result is already evident—a complicated, many-sided debate within and between the three countries on social, political, and economic issues. These issues do not exist in a vacuum. The prospects for approving and maintaining a free trade agreement will depend on an understanding of the psychological boundaries of integration.

MEXICAN LIMITS

Historically, the Mexican government has limited public debate on its policies. The governing party, the PRI, alternated its use of subtle and heavy-handed tactics to keep dissent within set boundaries. This is changing. The boundaries are moving to allow for greater freedom. One of the reasons that the system has begun to open is the legacy of the 1988 election. Whether Cuauhtémoc Cárdenas has a future in Mexico's politics or not, his place in history is assured by his defection from the ruling party. By leaving the PRI, he turned a private, internal party discussion into a public debate, making opposition legitimate and democracy possible. Although the PRI is not fully reconciled to public debate of controversial issues, the party has become aware of the cost of domestic censorship to its image internationally. It is also much harder to maintain a political wall when the social and economic walls are coming down.

It is also hard to understand the debate in Mexico because the traditional political spectrum has been scrambled. The terms—left, right, revolutionary, conservative—have lost much of their meaning in the substantive debate, although they retain their emotional charge. Cárdenas lays claim to the PRI's "revolutionary" tradition, and Salinas is accused of being "conservative." Yet Salinas defined an agenda of fundamental change, and Cárdenas has largely accepted it. When Cárdenas was asked whether he would reverse Salinas's program of privatization and freer trade and investment with the United States if he were elected president in 1994, he responded sharply: "I never said that."[2]

Pressed another time as to whether he would do it, Cárdenas said, "I would review the program on a pragmatic, not an ideological basis," rotating the terms of the debate to counter those who call him an ideologue and Salinas a pragmatist. His point is that Salinas has "indiscriminately" lowered the protective economic barriers without taking into account the social, political, or national security effects of his decisions. He argues that it is "irrational" to privatize state companies that are profitable.

To a question concerning which companies he would renationalize, Cárdenas again adeptly turned the tables: "The first thing I would do is privatize the media." The government took a few steps to do that in 1992, but "the real issue," Cárdenas said, "is at what speed, how deeply, and under what conditions the [Salinas] changes should be undertaken."[3] For a revolutionary, Cárdenas is surprisingly uncomfortable with the pace of change. His is a classically conservative defense of the status quo, a quibble rather than an alternative, but his comment reveals in a subtle way the maturing of Mexican politics.

Cárdenas stands astride a heterogenous, leftist popular movement. He admits that his major challenge is to transform his personal support into an institutional base for his Party of Democratic Revolution (PRD). Taking clear positions on economic policy risks fragmenting the coalition, which includes Marxists who are unalterably opposed to Salinas's reforms, his answers are clever ways to avoid the questions and preserve his options. Some businessmen believe Cárdenas would revive the old state-led model if he were ever to come to power, a prospect that they think is extremely unlikely since his and his party's fortunes have declined precipitously since 1988.

There is no doubt that he would use the state to intervene in the economy more than would Salinas, but if the current reforms work, he probably would make only modest changes. If they fail, the statist voices in his party would be strengthened, and he would likely listen to them and advocate a return to a more protectionist model. Unless the Mexican economy collapsed, or the trade pact was perceived as an unmitigated liability for Mexico, he probably would not repeal it, although he might try to restrict its impact and certainly would not contemplate expanding it. Cárdenas's ambiguity on these subjects permits him and the country to ground the new politics on results rather than on the empty slogans of the past. Salinas agrees that performance should be the standard: "Today . . . being progressive is measured by deeds and results, not by rhetoric."[4]

While Cárdenas insists that he wants respectful relations with the United States, he and his party are more suspicious and inclined to see the United States in a negative light. During the Persian Gulf War, while Salinas increased oil shipments to the United States, Cárdenas advised suspending sales to *all* combatants. His real target was clearly the United States. He resented the use of the United Nations by the United States for its own ends, saying: "We can't leave the fate of humanity in the hands and morals of the murderers of Grenada and Panama."[5] U.S. relations with a Cárdenas government would in all probability be similar to those in the pre-Salinas era, distant and more difficult, with small irritants often becoming major crises.

The contest between Salinas and Cárdenas has a larger significance for NAFTA and for the rest of the hemisphere because it defines the two ends of a crucial debate on how the state should manage its economy and how Latin America should relate to the United States and the world. At one end are the Salinista "first world modernizers," who prefer a leaner state that respects the efficiency of the market but tries to alleviate its adverse consequences. "Social liberalism" is the way that Salinas defines his political philosophy: the market allocates resources, but the government corrects for its malfunctions. Salinas maintains good relations with Latin America and the third world, but his principal goal is to seek entry into the first world. He also believes in negotiating hard but pragmatically with the United States.

At the other end are the Cardenista "third world progressives," who believe that a bigger state is the key to development, that the private sector is rapacious, incompetent, and possibly unpatriotic, and that the United States should be kept at arm's length. This approach will rely on political mobilization of the masses rather than the individual loyalties of citizens; it will seek alliances with third world nations to bring pressure on the United States and the industrialized world to change the international economic system. The "third world progressives" believe that Mexico can develop only if it reduces its dependence on the United States; Washington is likely to view this philosophy as defensive or unfriendly.

The question is whether advocates of this view could return to Los Pinos (Mexico's White House). The answer is not straightforward because the Mexican political system is in the midst of an awkward transition from a closed society to a more open one.

Prior to 1989, no opposition party had ever won a single state governorship in Mexico. Salinas has opened the system wide enough to permit the conservative National Action Party (PAN) to elect two governors. But Cárdenas's party is weak in both organization and support, and it did poorly in the midterm elections in August 1991. Despite some efforts by Salinas to compile a new voter registration list and clean up the procedures for counting votes, public opinion polls indicated that a plurality of Mexicans had no confidence in the registration list, and only 42 percent of the Mexican people believed their vote would be respected. That was an improvement over 1988, when only 23 percent said that their vote counted, but it still meant that the majority of the Mexican people thought that the government was manipulating the electoral system.[6]

The two main opposition parties, the National Action party (PAN) and the Democratic Revolutionary party (PRD)—as well as Mexican observer groups—have complained repeatedly of electoral fraud. In July 1992, the PRI claimed victory in Michoacan, but the PRD did not accept the results there and maintained a steady stream of protests until the PRI candidate stepped down and new elections were promised. On November 8, 1992, elections were held in four states, and in all four, the opposition protested fraud. Salinas found himself in a no-win situation. The PRI can either lose an election, or it can claim victory and encounter demonstrations until it acknowledges defeat. With the ruling party's credibility so badly impaired, the electoral process is not working.[7]

Salinas said that he wanted to manage the political opening to democracy deliberately so as not to jeopardize his economic program, but in fact the political system cannot be managed in the same way as the economy. The issue is whether the vote is respected or not. In his November 1, 1992, state of the nation report, Salinas recognized the need for more fundamental political reforms to secure the confidence of the opposition parties. Specifically, he called on all the parties to negotiate three reforms: to make transparent the sources of party funding; to place ceilings on the cost of electoral campaigns; and to devise procedures that will assure the impartiality of the media during the electoral process.[8]

The difficult question is whether a consensus on these reforms is possible in time for the 1994 presidential election. The opposition parties are skeptical about the government's sincerity in negotiating these issues, and it is true that Salinas continues to try to have it both ways. He calls for modernizing Mexico, and yet he trots out the old PRI arguments to discourage dissent. At the PRI's National Assembly in September 1990, he denounced "those of the opposition who denigrate the party inside the country and who have no political shame in criticizing the PRI and the government abroad . . . without caring about the damage that this attitude can cause to the country." He dismissed Cárdenistas as "allies of those who seek to trample on the national sovereignty." This is the way that nationalism used to be defined in Mexico in order to stifle debate. Cárdenas uses similar arguments to criticize Salinas for adopting policies that amount to a "renunciation by Mexico of its sovereign rights."[9]

"The past," as William Faulkner wrote, "is never dead; it's not even past." Mexico has one foot in an authoritarian, defensive past and the other in a more liberal, internationalist future. This is true of Salinas, who has moved Mexico's economy boldly forward even as he uses old habits in the political arena. And it is true of Cárdenas, who wants to democratize Mexico's politics but is more equivocal about opening the economy.

Those who fear that a more democratic Mexico could lead to a Cárdenas victory and a reversal of NAFTA miss the point. The greatest danger to NAFTA in Mexico is electoral fraud that could lead to political instability. A second threat is if the United States imposes onerous conditions on Mexico or is insensitive to Mexico's need for autonomy. American arrogance will always evoke a defiant Mexican response whether a Salinas or a Cárdenas is president. If NAFTA succeeds in promoting Mexico's development, then a Cárdenista resurgence might constrain the pace of integration, but it will not reverse it. Indeed, the more open the political contest, the more likely that a reform like NAFTA will set down roots in the Mexican body politic.

THE TWO SIDES OF THE U.S. DEBATE

The United States is also of two minds on the question of openness to the international economy: a confident mindset that takes risks to expand opportunities, and a more fearful one that seeks to conserve and protect the country's wealth or its jobs. From the Mexican perspective, American confidence has always bordered on the arrogant; Mexico has had little experience and less awareness of a United States that was uncertain of itself.

With an economy almost twenty-five times the size of Mexico's, the United States should have less to fear in a free trade agreement than Mexico. That explains why the idea was often proposed from the north and rarely considered in the south. But the truth is that the source of Mexico's defensiveness is not unique; Americans possess similar fears about loss of control or identity. The anxiety that greeted the prospect of a Japanese takeover of an American baseball team is one example. Seventy percent of the American people said that "something about it [Japanese purchases in the United States] bothers" them. Even as Mexico's fear of U.S. takeovers seems to have subsided, U.S. fears of Japanese and other foreign investments have increased. Two-thirds of the American people in a 1988 poll favored restrictions on foreign investment. The principal reasons are the same as have been given in Mexico and Canada: a desire for economic and political autonomy. Three-quarters of the people, according to a Louis Harris survey in 1988, agreed that "increased Japanese economic involvement in the United States could someday give the Japanese too much influence over U.S. government policies."[10]

While the Mexican "third world progressive" fears being overrun by U.S. companies, some Americans fear being overrun by Mexicans coming to the United States for work. Others fear abandonment by U.S. corporations going to Mexico to exploit cheap labor. Many fear that jobs will be lost and environmental and labor standards will be eroded by more integration. Some Americans believe that the concentration of Mexicans in the southwest could lead to a Quebec-like problem, and that the prevalence of Spanish in this region and elsewhere exacerbates that problem and threatens the unity of the country. Still another concern is Mexico's lack of democracy. Senator Daniel Patrick Moynihan, the new chairman of the Senate Finance Committee, explained that the reason he had "the strongest reservations about the free trade agreement with Mexico [was because it would be] the first free trade agreement we are being asked to consider with a country that isn't free."[11]

Each of these concerns has a psychological and a substantive dimension. To the extent that the substantive concerns are addressed effectively, the psychological worries diminish, but if the governments are unresponsive to the issues—employment, environment, immigration, human rights—then the underlying concerns are compounded. Sooner or later, words and policies give expression to the qualms of the populace. The debate in Mexico is affected by the public criticisms on the American side in a manner that strengthens the argument of the pessimists. If the United States rejects NAFTA, those Mexicans who insisted that the gringos can never be trusted will be proved right, and Mexico's defensive nationalists will be stronger. If Congress approves NAFTA and builds on it to facilitate Mexico's transition toward a modern economy, then it is likely to evoke more positive responses from Mexico.

CONVERGING AGENDAS AND ATTITUDES

The effect of the division within the PRI, together with dismantling the tariff walls, was to open up the debate in Mexico and connect it with the parallel one taking place in the United States. This bond was reinforced by the convergence of broad public attitudes in the two countries on domestic and international issues. The United States seems more concerned about the nontrade issues, but there are numerous groups in the three countries that share the same goals concerning the environment, labor standards, and democracy. It might be more accurate to state that Mexican groups are using the U.S. debate to enhance their bargaining leverage within Mexico than to argue that the United States is using NAFTA to press its agenda on a passive Mexico.

On environmental issues, for example, during the last decade, there has been a remarkable convergence of opinion in Canada, Mexico, and the United States. While less than one-quarter of Mexicans were concerned about environmental issues in 1982, more than two-thirds were worried in 1992—roughly the same proportion as Americans and slightly higher than in Canada. More significantly, in 1992, 72 percent of Mexicans wanted to protect the environment "even at the risk of economic growth," compared to 59 percent of Americans and 68 percent of Canadians.[12] So it is clear that the environmental movement in Mexico has grass roots.

The convergence of public opinion on social, political, and economic issues in the three counties extends considerably beyond environmental issues. Ronald Inglehart of the United States, Neil Nevitte of Canada, and Miguel Basañez of Mexico conducted surveys in all three countries at the beginning and at the end of the 1980s, and they found that attitudes are not only similar but that they also have been converging in a way that makes further integration more feasible.[13]

In all three countries, public attitudes increasingly support political liberalization, a free market (but *not* laissez-faire) economic policy, and a higher priority for autonomy and self-expression in all spheres of life. Still more important is the convergence in the values that parents are trying to instill in their children. When asked which of seventeen qualities people would like their children to have, respondents from all three countries chose the same qualities and even ranked them similarly. The authors of the study believe that the main cause of the convergence in value systems is that young people in all three countries are better educated and more influenced by global communications. "A narrow nationalism that had been dominant since the 19th century is gradually giving way to a more cosmopolitan sense of identity."[14]

This view is not widely held among the generation currently in power, and all three countries, of course, retain elements of a parochialism even as a more modern, North American orientation is becoming visible. The integration process will be helped along by the knowledge that both inward and outward perspectives lurk beneath the surface of the debate, and that the words and actions of one country can reinforce their counterparts in another. The three countries can shape their hopes together, or each can give in to its own fears.

Theories developed using the Western European experience suggest that increased economic interaction does not lead to political community *unless* there is an increase in trust—the trust that comes from shared experiences that reinforce positive feelings toward other peoples.[15] Polls in North America indicate that there is a high level of trust between the United States and Canada, and a slightly lower level of trust is shown by these two toward Mexico. But Mexicans are more likely to distrust Americans than trust them. Nonetheless, the experience of Europe shows that distrust can erode, as it did between the French and the Germans from the 1950s to the 1970s as a result of working together in the European Community.

In the case of North America, historical experience taught both Canada and Mexico to defend themselves against the United States and to prefer that relations be kept at a certain distance, but the Inglehart, Nevitte, and Basañez study discovered that those feelings have undergone a fundamental change. By 1990, Canadians and Mexicans were more inclined to support freer trade and closer ties to their neighbors than Americans. "To an astonishing extent, these traditional forms of nationalism seem to have vanished."[16] What has replaced nationalism is a cooperative realism; more than 80 percent of the public in all three countries favors freer trade *provided that it is fair and reciprocal*; 15 percent of people oppose it.[17] As support for economic integration in the three countries increases so too does support for political integration. Younger people particularly were nearly three times as likely to say they belonged to North America or to the world as were those in the oldest group.[18] Whether the path toward economic integration and political community is direct, bumpy, or circular depends to a great extent on how the three governments and peoples treat one another in the years ahead.

TRADE POLICY AND POLITICS

The debate on NAFTA within each country and between them is also shaped by the changing character of trade policy and the give-and-take of trade politics. To succeed, trade policy must bridge the contradictions between economic and political logic.

The economic logic follows from the trade theory of Adam Smith and David Ricardo: Free trade can benefit all nations if the market is permitted to allocate goods and services without tariffs or government distortions. Every economist learns this theory, and most are frustrated and befuddled that politicians seem not to have learned it and keep interfering with the free market, making everyone worse off.

Political logic begins from a different premise, namely, that people, firms, and unions are moved more by fear than by hope. Those who lose jobs because of cheaper imports have a greater incentive to press their views on Congress than those who owe their jobs to exports. The political implications are clear cut: if you lose, you want to blame someone else, and you seek redress from Congress. If you gain, you tend to believe that you alone are responsible.

The trade debate ricochets between these two logics. Professionals and interest groups tend to cluster around one or the other and argue past one another. Public opinion surveys conducted for the Chicago Council on Foreign Relations show that among the many foreign policy issues, trade policy is one that consistently reveals one of the largest opinion gaps between leaders and the American public, and between business and labor. In 1990, for example, 64 percent of leaders and 33 percent of the general public favored eliminating tariffs on imports; 78 percent of business executives felt tariffs should be eliminated, and 75 percent of labor leaders believed they should be maintained.[19]

Elected leaders have to mediate between these poles. If a congressman or senator represents a constituency that is suffering due to trade, he or she will tend to follow the political logic; representatives from prosperous areas will likely advocate freer trade. The role of the president in settling this debate is pivotal. The last president who hinted to Congress that he would protect U.S. companies was Herbert Hoover, and the disastrous Smoot-Hawley Tariff was the result. Since then, every president has weighed in on the side of freer trade, and as a result no protectionist measures have become law.[20] Nonetheless, the debate on trade is often very confusing because at any one moment there might be hundreds of protectionist *bills* moving through Congress. Representatives introduce these bills to send three messages: to constituents that they hear their pain; to the president that he needs to give higher priority to these issues; and to foreign countries that they need to open up their markets if they expect the United States to keep its market open to them. These bills always evoke a Newtonian equal-and-opposite reaction by the free-traders. This pattern can be called the "cry-and-sigh" syndrome because at the beginning of every congressional session a cry of protectionism is heard, but by the end the protectionist bills have failed, and one can hear sighs of relief.

The trade debate is also defined by the "fast-track" procedure by which Congress has to approve or disapprove the legislation implementing the NAFTA trade agreement within ninety days and without amendment. Incorporated in the 1974 Trade Reform Act, the fast-track procedure represented the second significant change in the way in which the United States makes trade policy. (The first occurred in the 1934 law that gave the president power to negotiate trade agreements.) The Constitution granted to Congress the responsibility for making trade policy, and, from 1789 until 1934, Congress did so by deciding on tariffs for each product. The Smoot-Hawley Tariff of 1930 included 20,000 amendments to raise tariffs on that many products. "I might suggest that we have taxed everything in this bill except gall," said Senator Thaddeus Caraway of Arkansas. "Yes," Senator Carter Glass of Virginia replied, "and a tax on that would bring in a considerable revenue."[21]

Smoot-Hawley exacerbated the U.S. and world depression and was such an unmitigated disaster that when President Franklin Roosevelt requested a new trade bill, Congress was prepared to accept an unprecedented transfer of power to the executive. In the 1934 law, rather than raise tariffs again, Congress delegated to the president the authority to lower them by negotiating reciprocal trade agreements. Since then, the argument for protection has become one of exception rather than principle. U.S. tariff barriers fell from an average of 59.1 percent in the early 1930s to less than 10 percent by 1972.[22]

By the 1970s, tariffs had been reduced to such a low level that they were no longer the main trade issue. They were replaced by nontariff barriers (NTBs), which are government policies that affect the flows of trade and investment. Some NTBs, like quotas and voluntary export restraint agreements, are aimed at impeding trade, but there are many other policies (for example, sales taxes or agricultural subsidies) that affect trade but are legislated for a different purpose. These NTBs moved to the center of the agenda in the Tokyo Round (1974–79) and the Uruguay Round (from 1986 onward) of trade negotiations, and they have proved to be very difficult to negotiate for both political and technical reasons.

Since NTBs are often domestic policies, Congress does not like to relinquish complete authority over them to the president's negotiators. The president, however, does not wish to negotiate NTBs, knowing that Congress could amend or delay ratification, to the irritation of our trading partners. The "fast-track" procedure was the compromise. The president would consult with Congress at every stage of the negotiations. When an agreement was reached, congressional aides would draft the implementing legislation with the president's trade representatives, and the bill would then be sent to Congress for a vote—with a deadline and with no amendments permitted.

With regard to NAFTA, the fast-track process affected the policy in two important ways. U.S. Trade Representative Carla Hills was required to consult with a host of advisory groups representing big and small business, labor, agriculture, retailers, consumer groups, and the general public. She astutely tried to satisfy as many of the private interests as possible in order to prevent a blocking coalition against the agreement. The business community strongly endorsed the agreement, while labor felt that few, if any, of its concerns had been addressed by U.S. negotiators. Most of the other groups fell somewhere in between in their degree of support for the agreement.

Putting the treaty on a fast track also denies Congress the chance to rewrite the specifics of the agreement to respond to the interests representing individual products or sectors. Instead, Congress has to decide on the agreement as a whole: Is NAFTA in the national interest of the United States? Yes or no?

The politics of international trade bears some similarities to that of domestic trade politics. Countries that are most fearful of foreign competition tend to set the boundaries and the pace of negotiations. Leaders of these countries wait for incentives from others to open their markets. The French president or the Japanese prime minister, for example, does not want to antagonize farmers just because the United States wants to open up other countries' agricultural markets. No progress is possible in these negotiations until the U.S. president gives these leaders a reason to act—either an incentive or more likely a potentially painful disincentive.

Sometimes, the United States has to make a credible threat that it will close its market to some of the offending country's exports, and the possible cost of that action has to exceed the economic and political price of protection for the country's farmers. Without such a prod, the negotiations would stalemate. It is hardly a coincidence that the Europeans finally began to take U.S. concerns with their agricultural subsidies seriously when the Americans promised to impose a 200 percent tariff on their wine. Similarly, Canada and Mexico both approached the United States for a free-trade agreement not because of their hopes for a larger market but because of fear of being arbitrarily shut out of the U.S. market.

Advocates of following strict economic logic condemn this process as inefficient and self-destructive; they rarely understand or appreciate the logic of politics. They think that if the United States threatens to close its market, it will get into a trade war, and everyone will lose. They do not understand the critical difference between a real war and a trade war. In a real war, where the stakes are high and a country's very existence may be threatened, retreat is difficult to accept until a country gives up all hope of victory, or the costs become unbearable. In a trade "skirmish," countries carefully calculate costs and benefits, and when the costs of maintaining one policy exceed the benefits, they change.

The time has come to rethink U.S. trade strategy. Japan and Europe are unlikely to open their markets at some political cost unless their leaders see that there is going to be more harm to them in not doing so. The only way that their political calculations can change is if successful exporters join the debate, and that will not occur until French wine makers or Japanese electronic firms realize that they will pay a price for their government's support of farmers.

Only by integrating the twin logics of economics and politics can the United States begin to fashion a trade policy that enjoys wider popular support. The president must keep the focus on lowering trade barriers, but he also needs to be responsive to the needs of workers, small businesses, and environmentalists in order to gain broad-based support for the policy. Internationally, the United States should press for further reductions of world trade barriers, and should do so in ways that increase the prospects of success rather than ratify the politics of paralysis. In this competition for more open markets, Mexico is our ally, but cooperation is only possible if the United States and Mexico devise a respectful relationship that reinforces integrationist forces.

CHAPTER 3

NAFTA: The Economic Dimension

On August 12, 1992, the trade ministers of Mexico, the United States, and Canada announced that they had reached agreement on a North American Free Trade Area. They presented a preliminary text of the agreement one month later, and initialed a final agreement on October 7 in San Antonio. The document contains twenty-two chapters and, including tariff schedules, runs to nearly two thousand pages. Of course, if it were really a *free* trade agreement, less than one page would be needed to eliminate all restrictions on trade. Instead, it is a *freer* trade agreement that promotes integration by reducing and eventually eliminating *most* trade and investment barriers and harmonizing policies on fair competition, trade in services, government procurement, and intellectual property rights. In addition, and in anticipation of its critics, the governments promise in the preamble of the agreement to "strengthen the development and enforcement of environmental laws and regulations; and protect, enhance and enforce basic workers' rights."

The market created by NAFTA is a formidable one. The combined gross product of the three countries of North America was $6.2 trillion in 1990, having grown from $560 billion in 1960. (See Figure 3.1, page 38.) The region's total exports grew much faster than the overall economy, from $28.4 billion in 1960 to $523.2 billion in 1990, while imports grew somewhat faster than that, from $23.6 billion to $659.6 billion. (See Figure 3.2, page 39.) Since 1986, U.S. exports to Mexico have increased three times faster than U.S. exports to the rest of the world.

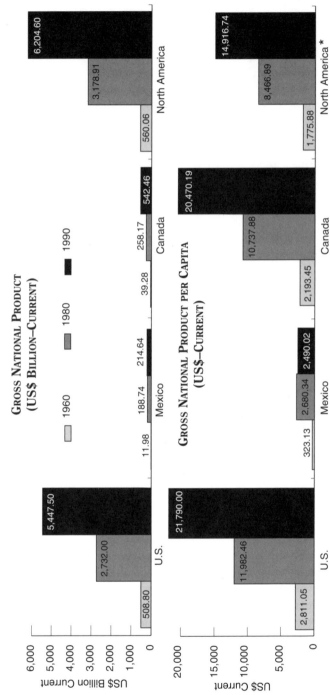

Figure 3.1
North America: Economic Indicators

Gross National Product
(US$ Billion–Current)

1960   1980   1990

Gross National Product per Capita
(US$–Current)

Sources: For this and Figure 3.2—The World Bank, *World Tables*, 1984, 1991; The World Bank, *World Development Report*, 1992; OECD, "Monthly Statistics on Foreign Trade," Paris, July 1992; and International Monetary Fund, *Direction of Trade Statistics Yearbook*, 1992.
*North American GNP per Capita is an average of the three countries.

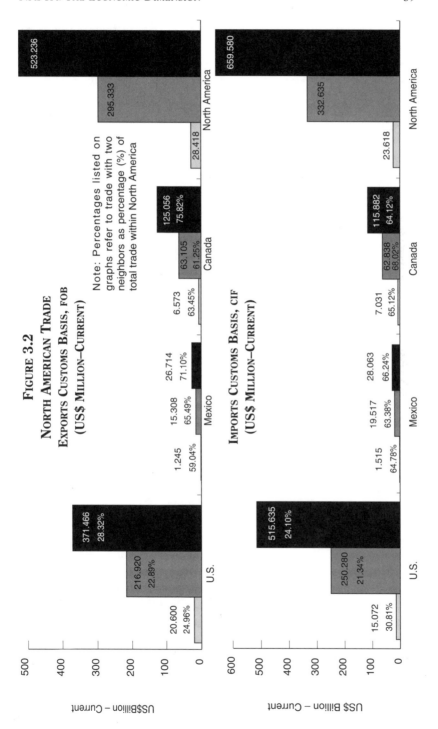

FIGURE 3.2
NORTH AMERICAN TRADE
EXPORTS CUSTOMS BASIS, FOB
(US$ MILLION–CURRENT)

Note: Percentages listed on
graphs refer to trade with two
neighbors as percentage (%) of
total trade within North America

IMPORTS CUSTOMS BASIS, CIF
(US$ MILLION–CURRENT)

The most important trading partners for each of the countries of North America are the others, although the degree of importance varies, with Canada and Mexico much more dependent on the U.S. market than the other way around. (See Figure 3.3.) But the North American market is also the most important for the United States—its two neighbors received 28.3 percent of total U.S. exports in 1990. Canada is the most important trading partner for the United States, and Mexico is third, although U.S. manufacturing exports to Mexico exceeded those going to Japan, its number two trading partner. The combined intraregional trade for North America represents about 40 percent of the three countries' total world trade.

Moreover, the potential for trade growth appears to be greater within North America, particularly where Mexico is concerned, than elsewhere. Every 1 percent increase in Mexico's rate of growth translates into $300 million more in U.S. exports or about 7,000 additional U.S. jobs.[1] Although the per capita income of Mexicans is about one-tenth of the level for Germans and Japanese, their per capita imports from the United States are worth roughly the same amount. (See Figure 3.4.) With Mexican trade barriers higher than those of the United States, the proposed reduction or elimination of the remaining restrictions presents real opportunities for U.S. exporters.

FIGURE 3.3
TRADE BALANCE
1991 IMPORTS AND EXPORTS
(US$ BILLIONS)

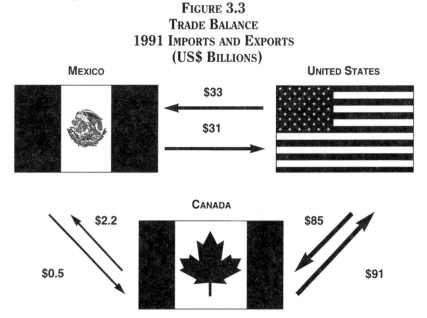

MEXICO

$33

$31

UNITED STATES

CANADA

$2.2

$0.5

$85

$91

Source: U.S. Department of the Census, Bureau of the Census, *Statistical Abstract of the United States*, various issues, 1950–1991 (Washington, D.C.: Government Printing Office).

FIGURE 3.4
IMPORTS FROM THE UNITED STATES PER CAPITA

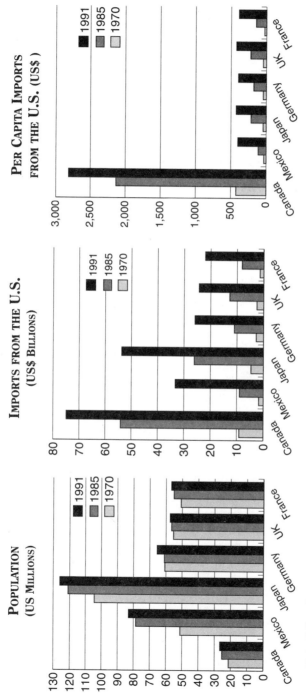

Note: If East German numbers are added to West German, 1991 population is 79.07 and 1991 per capita imports from the United States is 328.

Sources: The World Bank, *World Tables*, 1984, 1991; The World Bank, *World Development Report*, 1992; International Monetary Fund, *Direction of Trade Statistics Yearbook*, 1992; and U.S. Department of Commerce, *U.S. Merchandise Trade: Exports & Imports 1965–1976, 1977*.

Mexico's small GNP per capita compared with its neighbors may be more of an opportunity than a problem for the United States because of Mexico's potential for economic growth, as well as the burgeoning size of its population and its demographic complementarity with the United States. (See Figure 3.5, page 43.) The population of North America is 362 million, greater than the European Community. While immigration has been an important cause of the growth in population in the United States and Canada, improved health care has been the primary cause in Mexico.

Although the rate of population growth in Mexico has declined sharply in the period since the government introduced family planning in 1974, it is still about twice that of its two northern neighbors. The result is a much younger population in Mexico. In 1990, more than 36 percent of Mexico's population was under the age of fifteen and 3 percent were over the age of sixty, as compared to 20 percent under fifteen and 10-18 percent over sixty in the United States and Canada. As the population of the United States and Canada ages and begins to retire from the work force, Mexico's youth will enter it and, it is to be hoped, will both produce and consume more.

NAFTA PROVISIONS

The NAFTA agreement is a massive document that aims to reduce trade barriers at varying speeds and ways in different sectors. It is complicated in large part because it tries to integrate very unequal economies with diverse legal and regulatory systems. NAFTA will be phased in over a fifteen-year period in order to give additional time for "sensitive"— an interesting psychological word meaning noncompetitive—industries or farms either to become more competitive or to move into other lines of business. NAFTA broke new ground in trade negotiations. It was the first trade agreement that addressed the environmental issue by promoting the harmonization of standards on pollutants, eliminated quotas on textiles and apparel, created free trade in services (including the very large telecommunications area and the insurance market), and guaranteed total market access in agriculture, if only after a fifteen-year transition period.

TARIFFS. NAFTA provides for the progressive elimination of all tariffs. The average U.S. tariff on Mexican goods is 3.9 percent (2.5 percent for cars); the average Mexican tariff is 10 percent (20 percent on cars). Most tariffs will be eliminated when NAFTA comes into effect—January 1, 1994—or within five years. Tariffs on the most sensitive items will be phased

Figure 3.5
North America: Population and Profiles

Population

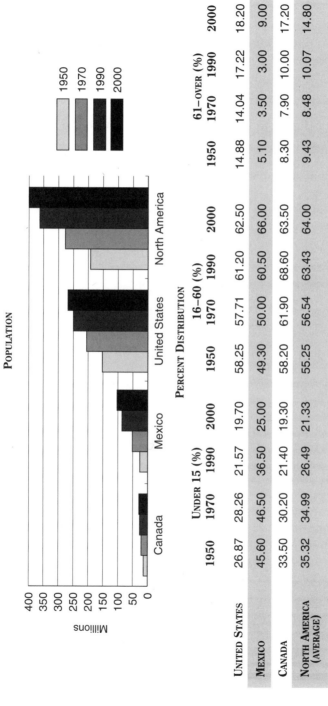

Percent Distribution

	Under 15 (%)				16–60 (%)				61–over (%)			
	1950	1970	1990	2000	1950	1970	1990	2000	1950	1970	1990	2000
United States	26.87	28.26	21.57	19.70	58.25	57.71	61.20	62.50	14.88	14.04	17.22	18.20
Mexico	45.60	46.50	36.50	25.00	49.30	50.00	60.50	66.00	5.10	3.50	3.00	9.00
Canada	33.50	30.20	21.40	19.30	58.20	61.90	68.60	63.50	8.30	7.90	10.00	17.20
North America (Average)	35.32	34.99	26.49	21.33	55.25	56.54	63.43	64.00	9.43	8.48	10.07	14.80

United States data for the year 2000 are projections from the U.S. Bureau of the Census; projections for Canada and Mexico are based on World Bank estimates.

Sources: U.S. Department of Commerce, Bureau of the Census, *Statistical Abstract of the U.S.*, 1991; and The World Bank, *World Tables*, 1984 and 1991, *World Tables-Social Data*, 1984, and *World Development Report*, 1992.

out during periods of up to fifteen years. Quotas and import licenses will be eliminated, but each country will retain the right to restrict trade to protect human, animal, or plant life, or the environment, *consistent with national treatment*. The last phrase means that a country cannot impose more stringent regulations on its neighbors' products than it does on its own. Special rules apply to agriculture, automobiles, energy, and textiles.

RULES OF ORIGIN. In order to deal with concerns that Japanese and other firms might use Mexico as a manufacturing platform for exports to the United States, NAFTA establishes strict formulas for rules of origin, which means that duties need to be paid on goods that derive a substantial portion of their value from labor, components, or materials that originate outside of North America. Strict rules apply to automobiles; 62.5 percent of the automobiles or their component parts would have to be made in North America. Although this exceeds the level established in the U.S.-Canadian agreement, both auto workers and companies wanted higher standards to prevent Japanese firms from sending their automotive components to Mexico for assembly. NAFTA has safeguard provisions to permit a country to raise its tariffs or barriers in the event of a surge of imports that "constitute a substantial cause of serious injury, or threat thereof, to a domestic industry."

AGRICULTURE. Virtually every government in the world protects its farmers from the vagaries of the weather and, to varying degrees, from international competition. In the Uruguay Round of multilateral trade negotiations, the United States and other countries with competitive agricultural sectors have aimed to reduce this protection substantially. The GATT negotiations were paralyzed for years, in large part because this objective was so difficult to achieve. NAFTA's negotiators can therefore take some pride in their progress in this area, although they needed to negotiate three bilaterals instead of a single agreement on agriculture. In principle, they agreed to eliminate all of the quotas and quantitative restrictions and 50 percent of all tariffs on the date NAFTA goes into force. In some cases, those quotas will be replaced by tariff-rate quotas (TRQs) that allow imports duty free up to a certain quota; above that, a tariff is paid. The remaining tariffs and TRQs will be phased out over a period ranging from five to fifteen years. The United States will use the longest period for sugar, peanuts, certain fruits and vegetables, and orange juice; Mexico will use it for corn, beans, and milk powder. NAFTA also established a trilateral committee to monitor the implementation of the agricultural provisions and to put in place special safeguards for certain fruits and vegetables to prevent surges of exports.

SERVICES. The service industry accounts for two-thirds of the U.S. economy but just one-fourth of U.S. exports to Mexico because of many restrictions on the exchange of services. With some exceptions, the agreement opens up both countries to "national treatment" and mutual recognition of licenses and certifications. In the area of transportation, NAFTA provides for a gradual phaseout of constraints on cross-border movements by car, truck, train, or ship. Mexico opens up to fair bidding most of its government purchases, but each government reserves certain areas for its own companies—for example, small businesses retain certain procurement rights in the United States. Ironically, the most restrictive element remaining does not involve Mexico; it is Canada's "cultural exemption," which limits the share of the U.S. entertainment industry in the Canadian television and film markets. In financial services, Mexico will eliminate most restrictions on foreign majority ownership of banks, securities firms, and insurance companies by the year 2000.

ENERGY. U.S. negotiators tried hard to get Mexico to open up its most sensitive area, oil and gas production. Periodic rumors that Mexico had sold its national patrimony compelled President Salinas to restate his commitment to the Mexican constitution's provision on state ownership of energy. Of all the elements in NAFTA, the one that evoked the greatest fears in Mexico and the sharpest disappointment among the U.S. business community was the energy sector. The business-oriented Advisory Committee for Trade Policy and Negotiations lectured Mexico that its future development required it to "overcome historical trepidations about removing outmoded, statist controls in important sectors such as energy." Its report said that "shortfalls in the agreement on energy [were] an unfortunate remnant of Mexico's isolationist past and in no way a precedent for future negotiations."[2] Although Mexican sensitivity about sovereignty could have caused any tactics perceived as strong-arming to backfire, U.S. pressure did have an effect. Mexico increased access to its electricity, petrochemical, gas, and energy services, and energy equipment markets.

INVESTMENT. Both Mexico and Canada reserved the right to screen foreign investment, although only if the value exceeded $150 million in Canada and $25 million in Mexico in 1994 (with the threshold rising to

$150 million in ten years). Mexico also agreed to end some performance requirements for new investors, for example, that they would have to export a certain amount.

INTELLECTUAL PROPERTY RIGHTS. NAFTA creates a durable regime to protect intellectual property rights for copyrights and patents. It also defines a common approach to prevent anticompetitive and monopolistic business practices.

IMMIGRATION. Just as Mexico tried to exclude energy from the negotiations, the United States sought to keep immigration off the table. In the end, all three sides agreed to permit the temporary entry of businessmen, but the United States decided to limit entry to 5,500 Mexican professionals.

ENVIRONMENT. NAFTA assures that U.S. sanitary, phytosanitary, and other environmental standards will be maintained and that all three governments will try to increase their standards to the highest level. It states that no government can relax its environmental standards in order to attract investment, and allows a local or state government to maintain higher than national standards provided they are not applied in a discriminatory manner.

DISPUTE-SETTLEMENT PROCEDURES. One of the reasons that Canada and then Mexico pursued a free trade agreement with the United States was that each feared being locked out of the U.S. market through arbitrary application of unfair trade laws, particularly on antidumping penalties and countervailing duties. NAFTA permits each country to retain its laws, but it allows each to seek reviews of the others' rulings on trade through binational panels that will make binding judgments. A country has the option of trying to reverse these decisions by requesting a three-person challenge committee.

NAFTA establishes in addition a North American Trade Commission composed of cabinet-level officers to assess complaints from each country concerning violations of the agreement. A secretariat will be provided for the staff work. If normal consultation fails to resolve a problem within forty-five days, then a country could call a meeting of the Trade Commission. If that fails, the country could ask for the convening of an Arbitral Panel of experts, either under GATT or NAFTA, which would issue a report within three months with recommendations for resolving the problem. If the parties do not accept the recommendations, then the country with the complaint can suspend the application of equivalent benefits—for example, by raising tariffs—until the issue is resolved. If the other country considers the retaliation excessive, it can seek another panel's recommendation.

ESTIMATED ECONOMIC IMPACT OF NAFTA

In assessing the potential impact of NAFTA on the economies of the United States and Mexico, one needs to recall that its purpose is to advance, not initiate, an integrative process that began with labor flows, accelerated with the increase in trade due to Mexico's economic liberalization, and has led to the development of a uniquely integrated border region and production-sharing industry.

President Bush's principal argument for welcoming the agreement on August 12 was that "it will create jobs and generate economic growth in all three countries." He noted that more than 600,000 Americans are now employed in jobs making or selling products to Mexico, and that export-related jobs pay 17 percent more than the average U.S. wage. The opening of the Mexican market, already the fastest-growing, will create new opportunities for U.S. exports. His secondary argument was that free trade will force American business to become more competitive.[3]

The most vigorous opponents of NAFTA are the U.S. labor unions. They argue that free trade with Mexico is a license for U.S. corporations to shut down plants nationwide and move their factories south to exploit cheaper Mexican labor. Businesses and farms that are already suffering from international competition also make similar arguments. Representatives of the labor unions issued a report in September 1992 condemning NAFTA as "inequitable and non-reciprocal" and declaring that it "would worsen the serious economic and social problems facing the United States."[4]

NAFTA is likely to lead to serious dislocation in certain labor-intensive industries, and fruit and vegetable farmers will find it difficult, perhaps impossible, to compete against Mexicans, although they will be granted considerable time to adjust. The issues for the nation are: *Will trade produce a significant enough net benefit, from both added exports and cheaper and better imports? Can public policies help those who lose their jobs?*

There is a long-standing debate as to whether jobs are lost in the United States because firms relocate across the border or whether jobs are secured supplying parts to the new plants that are set up in Mexico. There are cases to prove both points. A Commerce Department study found that materials used by maquiladora plants in Ciudad Juárez originated from 5,714 companies in 44 states; moreover, only 38 percent of the supplier firms were on the border.[5] U.S. firms that close down operations here may relocate to Tijuana or Taiwan, but Mexico purchases a much larger share of its imports from the United States than does Taiwan.

Some are concerned that U.S. investment in Mexico will be at the expense of investment at home, and that many firms that move production to Mexico will aim to export back to the United States the same goods that they had fabricated domestically beforehand. Undoubtedly this occurs, but one study found that 70 percent of U.S. investment in Mexico is aimed at developing the Mexican market. This is consistent with the pattern of most foreign investment globally. Roughly 75 percent of all U.S. foreign direct investment is in industrialized countries with wage levels comparable to those in the United States.[6] In the late 1980s, only 14 percent of the annual foreign direct investment flows went into developing countries; of that, nearly two-thirds went to seven countries, one of which was Mexico. The principal characteristic of these countries was that they had large internal markets, which could not be serviced by exports as well as by local manufacturers.[7] In brief, U.S. investment abroad is not always at the expense of investment at home. In some cases, it can promote additional jobs at home by using American capital goods or technology to establish a plant or other facilities for assembling goods.

To estimate the potential effect of NAFTA, economists have used a wide variety of computable general equilibrium (CGE) models.[8] Some of these models examine the effect on the entire U.S. and Mexican economies; others concentrate on particular sectors. Some are static and some dynamic in trying to measure the effect of reduced trade barriers on trade, growth, investment, and other economic variables. The specific results of each model depend on the assumptions that each uses and the variables—number of sectors, time frame—employed.

Four separate studies estimated that total job loss through plant closings and dislocation might range from 19,000 to 900,000. However, the Labor Advisory Committee, led by Thomas R. Donahue of the AFL-CIO, estimated a narrower range; 290,000 to 550,000 jobs would be lost through the end of the decade.[9] These estimates vary widely because they use very different assumptions as to how various occupational sectors will respond to competition. However, taking into account that 55,000 *net* jobs were created each week in 1989, the highest estimate of permanent job loss over an extended period is not so high. It would be the equivalent of less than four months' net job growth in 1989, a year of modest economic expansion.[10] Moreover, the number of new jobs estimated to have been created as a result of the *expansion* of U.S. exports to Mexico from 1986 to 1991 was 420,000.[11]

Despite important differences between these models, there are several points of consensus—"a surprising degree of unanimity," according to the International Trade Commission.[12] First, the impact of NAFTA is estimated to be positive for all three countries in terms of increased trade, investment, employment, and growth. Second, the dynamic gains far outweigh the static ones, meaning that a sustained high rate of growth in Mexico would expand North American trade with widespread benefits for the entire continental economy; even "aggregate real wages of U.S. workers would rise."[13] Third, Mexico would gain most because its economy is the smallest and most dependent on trade with the United States. Estimated increases in real GDP for Mexico as a result of NAFTA alone range from 0.1 to 11.4 percent. Over a twenty-five-year period, the dynamic effects are predicted to produce gains of about 50 percent in Mexico's real GDP.

The Mexican economy is only 4 percent of the size of the U.S. economy, and its exports are about 6 percent of total U.S. imports. Therefore, the overall effect of NAFTA on the United States is not expected to be very large. The models estimate that NAFTA would cause the U.S. GDP to expand by 0.5 percent or less per year. The impact would be still smaller for Canada because of its limited trade with Mexico.

Since most of the studies were concluded before NAFTA was completed, the authors had to make some assumptions about what the agreement would do. Those studies that assumed a reduction in tariffs only yielded a much lower rate of gain than those that also assumed a reduction in nontariff barriers. The positive effects were also larger for those estimates that took into account NAFTA's impact on capital flows—particularly on investment in Mexico. Since NAFTA reduces and will eventually eliminate nontariff barriers, and since Mexico has liberalized its foreign investment law, the benefits of NAFTA are expected to be toward the high end of the estimates.

The model developed by Gary Hufbauer and Jeffrey Schott of the Institute for International Economics (IIE) relied less on theoretical assumptions and more on the actual trade liberalization experience of Mexico and other countries. Focusing on the period from 1989 to 1995, they projected an 11.2 percent annual rise in the volume of trade, which would raise Mexico's exports to $62.2 billion by the end of the period. If NAFTA were rejected, Mexico's exports would be $10.3 billion less than this.[14] Imports would be $78.1 billion in 1995—$22.3 billion more than if there were no NAFTA. Capital inflows would be $16 billion, of which $3.9 billion would be remittances from relatives up north.

Assuming Mexico would buy and sell goods to the United States at roughly the same level as it has, the United States would sell $16.7 billion more annually and buy $7.7 billion more in 1995 than it would without NAFTA. Assuming nearly 20,000 net jobs are created for each $1 billion in net exports, the difference between the 316,000 new jobs created and the 145,000 jobs lost due to increased competition would be 171,000. The job displacement figure of 145,000 over a five-year period should be juxtaposed with the total number of jobs displaced from 1985 to 1990 (8.9 million). In other words, NAFTA would have a trivial negative effect on the overall economy.[15]

The Hufbauer-Schott analysis is based on aggregate trade figures. A more precise analysis would focus on each sector, taking into account the transition schedules in NAFTA. That has not been done yet, but, again, such analyses would have to make assumptions on investment that would be very speculative, and perhaps would not yield any better estimates than the Hufbauer-Schott study. Nonetheless, given the overall size of the U.S. economy in relation to the changes in Mexico, almost all of the analyses agree that NAFTA's impact on the United States would not be large.

There is substantial agreement as to which sectors in each country would benefit and which would lose from freer trade, although there are discrepancies with respect to the magnitude of the gain or pain. The United States is expected to benefit from additional exports of field crops (wheat, corn, soybeans, rice), poultry, pork, processed foods, chemical intermediate products (rubber goods, pharmaceuticals, plastics), capital goods, transportation equipment, and automobiles. Mexicans will gain by exporting more fruits and vegetables, sugar, refined petroleum, textiles, and durable goods.

Gains by one country do not necessarily mean losses by the other, but in many "sensitive" sectors that will be the case, although the harm is spread out over long transition periods before all of the barriers are removed. Over the long term, one would expect that Mexico will not be able to compete against U.S. field crops, and the United States will not be able to compete against Mexico's fruit and vegetables. U.S. jobs will continue to be adversely affected in those industries that have already suffered serious job loss—automobile and auto parts, electronics, textiles, apparel, food processing, furniture, and glass. Additional trade in both directions is anticipated in metals (iron, steel, nonferrous metals, and fabricated metal, with U.S. exports of high-grade steel and U.S. imports of commercial-grade and construction steel increasing), textiles, machinery, and electronics.[16]

A study by the Office of Technology Assessment (OTA) concludes that the short-term impact of NAFTA will be favorable to the United States. Since the U.S. market is already relatively open compared to Mexico's, the immediate drop in Mexican trade barriers will stimulate continued growth in U.S. exports. Nonetheless, workers in apparel, auto parts, and television-assembly factories will lose jobs as these firms continue to close or relocate elsewhere, including Mexico. Over the longer-term—say fifteen years—however, much will depend on how the U.S. government manages the integration. If it repeats the policies of the last decade, the OTA concluded that less educated workers in the United States will continue losing about 1 percent of their real wages annually. The adoption of effective labor and industrial policies to promote research, encourage investment, and defend workers' rights, however, "could enable U.S. workers to enjoy 1 or 2 percent increases in living standards over the next 15 years. Mexico could grow at the 5 to 10 percent annual pace of developing Asian nations such as Thailand."[17]

MEXICAN DEVELOPMENT AND IMMIGRATION

The Bush administration claimed that NAFTA would promote development and stability in Mexico and reduce pressures for Mexicans to emigrate to the United States. Although many small businesses have folded because of the increased competition from firms both at home and abroad as a result of liberalization, Mexico's overall economic growth in the last three years has been impressive.

No one has disputed that NAFTA will foster Mexico's economic development in the long term, although the type of development likely to take root has been debated. Some fear that foreigners—particularly Americans—will gain control of the economy; others that small businesses will be driven out by large multinational corporations. Whether these fears come true will depend on the kinds of policies the Mexican government adopts.

The Hufbauer-Schott model estimates that 609,000 jobs would be created in Mexico, representing about 2 percent of total Mexican employment in 1995. There would be an 8.7 percent gain in Mexican real wages, a significant boost. Increased foreign investment is expected to generate higher-wage manufacturing jobs in Mexico, but perhaps not as many as some expect. With trade barriers gone, foreign investors will probably export their state-of-the-art technology, which uses less labor than older factories needed.

Increased development is commonly supposed to reduce emigration, but the assumption is incorrect. In fact, the pressures for emigration will probably increase in the short term, particularly as Mexican agriculture is reorganized and people leave rural areas for the cities, often the first stage for their journey north to the United States. The United States will grow in importance as a human magnet for Mexican workers. The main motive for emigration is not lack of jobs but the income differential, and it will be decades before Mexico's wage level begins to approach that of the United States.[18]

CHAPTER 4

THE NEW ISSUES OF INTERDEPENDENCE:
AN ANALYSIS

From the outset of the negotiations, all three governments insisted that the agenda was confined to trade and investment, with President Salinas being the most adamant that NAFTA was about "economic, not political integration."[1] Nonetheless, because of congressional pressure, the U.S. government was compelled to negotiate a wider range of issues, including the environment, workers' rights, health standards, and human rights. These issues had never been the subject of a comprehensive trade negotiation before. The Bush administration described them as "flank" issues, intending that they remain outside of the agreement. But congressional leaders insisted that if they were not dealt with effectively, ratification would not occur.

Both the United States and Mexico grappled with the substance of these new issues of interdependence and the appropriate procedures for dealing with them. This chapter will examine three sets of issues: the environment and border development, the social agenda (workers' rights, health standards, occupational safety), and human rights and democracy.

ENVIRONMENT AND BORDER DEVELOPMENT

During the last two decades, the environmental movement has grown in power and reach, affecting the calculations of an increasing number of businessmen and government officials throughout the world. Some "greens" have come to view the international trading system as a source of environmental problems due to "competing ideologies." Whereas environmentalists want to restrict and regulate development, advocates of freer trade try to eliminate regulations and barriers that inhibit the flow of goods and services.[2] Some environmentalists brook no compromise; they see free trade as a new form of colonialism. If NAFTA and GATT advance, Edward Goldsmith writes, "human, social, and environmental imperatives will be ruthlessly and systematically subordinated to the purely selfish, short-term financial interests of a few transnational corporations." These environmentalists' prescription is "not to increase the freedom of commercial concerns but . . . to bring those concerns back under control—to limit the size of markets, rather than expand them; to give local people control of their resources, not hand them over to the transnationals."[3]

It is Mexico's fate that its free trade proposal has collided with the environmentalists' new interest with trade. Most greens do not take as absolutist a view as Goldsmith, and, indeed, they are groping for the right formula to balance the interest of preserving the environment with that of promoting trade and development.[4] A sign of such flexibility was the decision by the National Wildlife Federation, an important U.S. environmental group, to support the fast-track negotiating authority after President Bush assured them he would take their concerns into account.[5] The environmental movement is not monolithic.

There are three sets of environmental issues of concern to the United States and Mexico: (1) border issues; (2) standards—specifically, whether lower standards or lax enforcement in Mexico will encourage U.S. corporations to relocate, causing a loss of American jobs and possibly a lowering of environmental standards in the United States; and (3) global concerns related to the destruction of the rain forest, the health-threatening pollution in Mexico City, the degradation of land, and the loss of plant and animal life.

In terms of NAFTA, "global concerns" take lower priority than the other two. Nonetheless, it is worth noting that at the U.N. Conference on the Environment and Development in Rio de Janeiro in June 1992, President Salinas announced a $200 million reforestation and air pollution control plan for Mexico, to be funded primarily through a debt-for-nature swap administered by the Inter-American Development Bank. Mexico's decision to postpone the building of a large dam because of its implications for the rain forest is another positive sign of government awareness of global environmental concerns.[6]

Some greens believe that international law should prescribe the same solutions for all communities, but Hufbauer and Schott argue cogently for the need to accept local priorities based on different needs and requirements. Los Angeles and Mexico City, for example, have compelling needs to limit auto emissions whereas Montana and Alberta, with different ecological concerns, would give higher priority to keeping their rivers clean.

Border environmental problems are primarily the result of an explosion in the growth in the last decade of the maquiladora industry and the corresponding increase in population. Rapid industrialization overburdened a thin infrastructure, and improper or inadequate waste treatment and air and water pollution created serious health hazards. The National Wildlife Federation identified the border pollution issue as its highest priority in U.S.-Mexican environmental relations, and the data support that conclusion. At Laredo, 25 million gallons of raw sewage flow into the Rio Grande every day. Contamination levels are 1,650 times greater than those considered safe for recreational use. In San Elizario, Texas, where an aquifer shared with Mexico has been contaminated, 35 percent of the children contract hepatitis A by age eight, and 90 percent of adults have had it by thirty-five.[7] Numerous reports confirm the multitude of health and environmental problems in the region.[8] In Brownsville, Texas, there were reports that babies were born with birth defects because of toxic waste disposal, but a systematic analysis by the Centers for Disease Control suggested that the defects were probably due to malnutrition. The level of incidence was high for Texas but not for communities on the Mexican side of the border.[9]

No one, least of all the people on the border, disputes the seriousness of the environmental problems. The questions that bear directly on the case for NAFTA are: whether the discrepancy in environmental standards serves as a magnet to attract U.S. companies to Mexico and, by doing so, encourages U.S. communities to lower their standards, leaving both countries environmentally worse off than before; whether NAFTA will accelerate this process; and whether the United States can assist Mexico in improving the protection of the border environment.

Stories of furniture companies in Los Angeles that moved to Mexico to escape tough local pollution laws were mentioned several times in the congressional debate as an indication of what might happen if NAFTA were approved.[10] The General Accounting Office conducted a study of this problem and found that between 11 and 28 furniture manufacturers in the Los Angeles area relocated to Mexico between 1988 and 1990, affecting approximately 960 to 2,547 jobs. About 83 percent of the companies mentioned the differences in wages and workers' compensation as the major motive for relocating; 78 percent also cited stringent environmental controls. *However, only 1 to 3 percent of the total number of furniture manufacturers in the Los Angeles area left, affecting only 2 to 10 percent of the jobs of local furniture workers.* The percentages shrink to insignificance if all furniture manufacturers in the United States are included.[11] The anecdotal evidence of furniture firms clearly does not tell the whole story.

Studies of the decisionmaking process of U.S. corporations that invest abroad reveal that environmental considerations have been negligible or nonexistent.[12] Other studies found little evidence that the costs of pollution abatement equipment influenced decisions on where industries move. Gene Grossman and Alan Krueger found that the costs involved in complying with environmental laws "are small in relation to the other components of total cost that determine whether it is profitable to operate in the United States or Mexico."[13] Mexico's comparative advantage is low wages, not lax environmental regulations. A second, more general study found that the weighted average cost-to-output of pollution abatement and control equipment was less than 1 percent of the total cost of doing business, and the highest costs for pollution control were just over 3 percent of the total. These numbers are simply too low to be considered an incentive for relocation.[14]

With regard to the possible effect of NAFTA on border development and pollution, two studies suggest that the border is likely to grow faster if NAFTA is rejected than if it is approved.[15] The main reason for this apparent paradox is that the maquiladoras, which rely on a partial exemption from tariffs, theoretically would become obsolete if tariffs were eliminated on trade between the two countries. The only reason for future investments to remain near the border is proximity, but there are many more important reasons why investors would prefer to locate further south. First, average wages in the maquiladoras are "considerably higher than in the interior of the country."[16] This is partly because of the extremely high turnover of workers, who often just stop in a maquila to earn enough money to pay a "coyote" to help them cross the boder into the United States, where they can earn many times as much.[17]

Second, the environmental and infrastructural problems are much worse on the border. The Mexican government already discourages investment in Mexico City and other congested urban areas, and as it implements more stringent environmental restrictions on the border area, firms will look to invest in the interior. Moreover, the government already provides incentives to investors to set up plants in "priority zones" that need development, and these are not near the border. In brief, NAFTA is likely to reduce the environmental problems on the border by eliminating the main incentive to invest there.

Environmental regulations and enforcement on the border and elsewhere in the country have changed drastically in the last four years. In 1988, the Mexican government passed the General Law for Ecological Equilibrium and Environmental Protection, its first environmental law. Modeled on the U.S. Environmental Protection Act of 1970, the law prohibits air, water, and soil pollution and contamination by hazardous waste, pesticides, and toxic substances. In some ways, Mexico's law goes beyond U.S. laws, for example, by requiring an environmental impact statement (EIS) on any investment involving hazardous waste. The U.S. requires an EIS only for projects with some public financing.[18]

The new law, however, was not enforced actively until Salinas's inauguration. Since talks began for NAFTA, in particular, Mexico's environmental efforts have accelerated, particularly in Mexico City and along the border. The environmental budget increased by a factor of nine in two years, and the number of environmental inspectors increased from nineteen in 1989 to one hundred in 1991, with half of those assigned to the border. Salinas granted additional resources to environmental matters in 1992 when he created the Secretariat of Social Development (SEDESOL) to relate environmental concerns more directly to a wider range of social responsibilities of the government. The environmental budget for the border area was increased by 450 percent, and the number of inspectors there was quadrupled to two hundred.[19] These new inspectors have closed 980 industrial sites, 82 of them permanently. The most spectacular example of the new commitment to environmentalism was the decision by Salinas to close a large oil refinery on the outskirts of Mexico City—at a cost of $500 million and 5,000 jobs. Within Mexico City, the government has gradually replaced the old gas-spewing buses, prohibited private cars from driving in the city one day a week, and required cleaner-burning gasoline.[20]

The pollution problems on the border are not as bad as in the capital, but they have a greater impact on the United States. The people on the border have a long history of trying to solve common problems while avoiding directives from their central governments.[21] One institution that has been very effective in working on sensitive trans-border problems, including water resources and sanitation, is the International Boundary and Water Commission, which was established more than one hundred years ago and reorganized in its current form in 1944. U.S. and Mexican environmental agencies have been working together on border issues since the "La Paz" agreement was signed in 1983. The problem with that agreement was that it was too general to be effective; it said nothing about enforcement, and it did not address the region's growing shortage of fresh water.[22]

It is clear that NAFTA injected life into environmental cooperation across the border. On February 12, 1992, after conducting many hearings among groups in both countries and circulating a draft, the two governments presented a three-year integrated plan for cleaning up the border. President Bush pledged nearly $379 million in fiscal years 1992 and 1993 that included funding for three waste treatment projects. Mexico promised to spend $466 million over three years, to work closely with the EPA to train border environmental inspectors, and to develop data bases that could be used by both sides.[23]

In a comprehensive analysis of the plan, Jan Gilbreath Rich of the University of Texas commended it as "the first large-scale attempt to integrate the planning and environmental strategies used by the two federal governments and a first attempt to recognize the direct link between natural resources and trade." The integrated plan dealt with many of the problems that had been overlooked by the agreement of 1983, but it promised more than its budget and personnel could possibly deliver, and many of the projects lacked specific implementation plans. Rich writes that the plan was conceived *because of NAFTA*, but, ironically, it deals with today's problems rather than the ones that will be faced after NAFTA comes into effect. Another irony is that Mexico pledged more resources to it than the United States. The U.S. federal government moreover promised state resources over which it has no control.[24]

Some environmentalists argue that any growth at all is damaging to the environment. Grossman and Krueger tested this hypothesis by comparing environmental pollution to levels of economic development worldwide, and they concluded that pollution is worse for low-income countries. As a country develops, it passes a certain threshold where it begins to shift resources toward a cleaner environment. Their formula suggests the threshold occurs when a country's per capita gross domestic product reaches $5,000. Since Mexico's income is near that level (in terms of purchasing power), one could expect new environmental investments in Mexico as long as its economy continues on its recent path of expansion.[25] In contrast with Mancur Olson's view that interest-group resistance to collective action increases as a country develops, thus inhibiting further growth,[26] Grossman and Krueger argue powerfully that interest group efforts *on behalf of collective choice* increase as an economy develops and the environment becomes polluted. Such public choices, they say, improve the prospects for further growth. The increasing clout of groups advocating a cleaner environment in Mexico seems to confirm their thesis. If external resources can be mobilized to supplement Mexico's in the battle against pollution, then the $5,000 threshold might well be reduced.

Although the Bush administration had insisted that it would address environmental issues on the "flank" of NAFTA, effective lobbying pressure compelled it to include important language in the text of the agreement itself. The chapters on Standards and Sanitary and Phytosanitary Measures allow states and cities to enact stricter standards than apply nationally or internationally, and they encourage the governments to harmonize their standards upward. Some environmental groups were pleased that NAFTA is adopting a more flexible scientific test for evaluating the merit of standards than currently exists in GATT, and that it places the burden of proof on the country challenging rather than the one defending the standard. Moreover, NAFTA deals explicitly with the "pollution haven" issue in the chapter on investment, which discourages countries from "derogating from" existing standards to "attract or maintain" investment, and in its call for the countries to consult with each other in the event of a complaint.[27]

Despite this very real progress, there are a number of omissions from the text that could undermine the agreement's effectiveness. The most important problem is that many of the provisions—for example, on pollution havens—are not tied to the dispute settlement mechanism, and consequently there is no mechanism for the United States to ensure that Mexico enforces its new pollution control laws. In a Congressional hearing on NAFTA, Representative Robert Matsui from California said, "Essentially, what the agreement now provides is a chance for Mexico to wink and not enforce its own laws and attract our business."[28] On September 17, 1992, perhaps in response to some of these concerns, the environment ministers of the United States, Mexico, and Canada agreed in principle to create a North American Commission on Environmental Cooperation to oversee the environmental aspects of the agreement. But the new group begs the old question: What will be done to make sure environmental standards are maintained?

Another difficult issue that was omitted from NAFTA was the appropriate basis for regulatory standards. Countries establish *product standards* to keep out goods that do not meet their level of safety or environmental quality—for example, some pesticides. The tough question is whether a country should be able to set standards on the *process* by which goods are produced—for example, preventing tuna from being imported if its harvest involved killing dolphins, or preventing a food from being imported if the farmers used a banned pesticide, even if there are no traces on the food. This is more of a moral or an economic issue than strictly one of trade. Thus, its applicability in a trade forum is a source of controversy. If an industry does not have to maintain the same level of environmental standards in Mexico as in the United States, then an American could argue that Mexicans have given a hidden subsidy to that industry. It is to be hoped that the logic of this argument will move the governments toward harmonizing their standards.

Provided that the integrated plan is implemented seriously and effectively, NAFTA might prove to be an environmental boon for both countries. Still, these issues need to be monitored. Betty Ferber de Aridjis, spokesperson for the Group of 100, Mexico's main environmental group, noted: "Plant closings [in Mexico] tapered down dramatically after the U.S. Congress approved fast-track procedures."[29] A General Accounting Office report in September 1992 showed that, despite the increasing environmental requirements in Mexico, most U.S. companies there did not file the requisite environmental impact statements. The Mexican agency responsible for environmental monitoring also acknowledged that of the 8,756 plants (a sample of 8.6 percent in the country) they had inspected, violations should have closed 418 and temporarily shut 1,909,[30] but these plants were given more time to correct their problems. Mexico has a long way to go. Nonetheless, when one compares the progress that Mexico has made in the four years since enactment of its environmental law with what the United States has accomplished in the two decades since passage of E.P.A., it is hard to avoid the conclusion that NAFTA has already had a profound and positive effect on the environment in Mexico.

Raising Mexico's environmental standards also has beneficial consequences for U.S. and Canadian exports of environmental technology. The environmental technology market in the United States has grown rapidly to about 2 percent of gross domestic product, or $160 billion.

The Mexican industry is growing faster from a much smaller base. The Mexican market for solid-waste-handling equipment alone, according to the U.S. Department of Commerce, will reach $625 million in 1992, and will continue to grow at a rate of 25 percent each year after that.[31] Some believe that cooperation on environmental matters could improve steadily after NAFTA, and they point to a precedent—the acid rain agreement between the United States and Canada was reached after the trade agreement.[32]

Even if NAFTA results in a reduction in foreign investment near the border, cross-border commerce will certainly expand, and the border area will have to absorb and adapt. The area is wealthier than much of Mexico, but much poorer than most of the United States. As such, it poses a special problem for the United States that extends beyond environmental concerns to issues of public health, education, and law enforcement. What is needed is a comprehensive approach to community development in the border area to improve the living standards of thousands of people who live in the colonias and lack basic services and minimal health conditions.[33] NAFTA does not address this issue at all.

THE SOCIAL AGENDA

Although the three governments were reasonably responsive to legitimate concerns raised by environmental groups, NAFTA reflects few of the concerns raised by U.S. labor unions. Indeed, there is a stark difference beween NAFTA's exquisite detail on investment rules and intellectual property rights and the absence of any language or credible program on workers' rights.

There are four sets of issues on the "social agenda": food health and safety standards, occupational safety and health, workers' standards, and training and adjustment assistance. Of these, only the first is dealt with adequately in NAFTA, which promotes the harmonization of strict health and safety regulations on food exports.

Like the environmental issues, the principal problems on the social agenda stem less from differences on policy than from an absence of political will in both the United States and Mexico and a gap in the capabilities (resources, trained personnel) of the Mexican state to enforce its own laws. In the area of occupational safety and health, President Bush, as part of his pledge to Congress, instructed the U.S. secretary of labor to sign a memorandum of understanding with her Mexican counterpart to provide for collaborative activities. The memorandum pledged to promote "higher living standards, and a safe and healthy workplace with adequate social security, medical, and financial benefits." The two governments then drafted a document that describes the two nations' systems, but it did not make the document available to the public or even to the unions. Conferences were held, but according to the AFL-CIO, "there has been absolutely no follow-up." The unions concluded that "the Administration has focused almost exclusively on description and other similar academic exercises, and has chosen not to develop any plans to address known problems in a meaningful way."[34]

In general, the occupational and safety conditions are probably better in the maquiladora industry, and in U.S. corporations in Mexico generally, than in most Mexican firms,[35] although there are important exceptions. Electronic assembly plants, for example, have been negligent in protecting their workers or the neighborhoods where they are located from toxic materials used in the production process.

One of the obstacles to protecting the safety of the workplace in Mexico is the lack of reliable or comprehensive data on the prevalence of work-related injuries or deaths. The International Labor Office (ILO) publishes cross-national statistics, but it has complained about the paucity and unreliability of much of the Mexican data. Nonetheless, ILO data from the late 1980s suggest that the Mexican fatality rate per million insured worker-hours is 0.12, which is roughly four times as high as the 0.03 rate for U.S. workers.[36]

Although the U.S. and Mexican labor movements have had close relations over many years, they disagree on whether NAFTA should be approved because both think the United States will lose jobs to Mexico. Efforts by American labor leaders to persuade their Mexican counterparts to negotiate a transnational "social charter" have therefore met with disinterest or silence.

A second reason that the dialogue between the two labor movements has been mute is that they relate to their governments in very different ways. The labor-government relationship in the United States has been at arm's length, sometimes cooperative but more often adversarial, particularly when Republicans occupy the White House. Although labor is one of the Democratic party's principal constituent groups, the differences between the party and the unions are much wider than between Mexican labor and the PRI-dominated Mexican state. Thus, the endorsement by Democratic president Bill Clinton of NAFTA, despite the vigorous opposition by unions, does not strike Americans as unusual.

The enormous Confederation of Mexican Workers (CTM) claims a membership of 5 million people, representing 90 percent of all industrial workers. It is ostensibly stronger than U.S. unions, but in fact the CTM's power is more limited because of the nature of its bargain with the state. This bargain has prevented any rival unions from competing with the CTM; in turn, the union has moderated demands for wage hikes and kept strikes to a minimum. Since December 1987, CTM support for the "solidarity pacts" negotiated by the state, labor, and management—which compelled labor to sustain a cut in real wages—permitted Mexico to shrink its inflation.

In terms of labor standards, this interdependent relationship has produced a more comprehensive set of legal protections for workers than in most countries with comparable levels of development. "In many respects," writes Tom Barry, "Mexico has one of the most advanced labor laws on the continent, largely as a result of the Mexican Revolution."[37] Indeed, Mexico's social legislation has more in common with Europe's than with the United States'. The labor laws contain elaborate guidelines on collective bargaining, the right to strike, rights regarding dismissal, an eight-hour day, housing benefits, vacations, profit sharing, a minimum wage, social security benefits, child care, and health services. A comparison of U.S., Mexican, and Canadian labor laws suggests that U.S. labor unions would benefit the most from a harmonization of standards. Unlike Mexico and Canada, the U.S. government does not require paid vacations or maternity leave (Mexico provides six months; Canada, seventeen weeks), and the United States is alone in permitting businesses to hire nonunion replacement workers during a strike.[38]

The irony is that while American unions fear the decline of their labor standards as a result of NAFTA, the opposite is happening. Mexican labor standards are sinking to the American level. Among the "reforms" being considered by Mexican unions are the removal of the government's role in protecting workers' rights, converting the daily shift and wage scales into an hourly measurement, giving preferences to nonunion workers, restricting the right to strike, and giving employers more leeway to lay off workers.[39] All of these steps would give Mexican firms the same kind of flexibility that their American counterparts have by taking away exisiting protections from union members. There are some signs of increasing unrest among workers, however. These "reforms" have already provoked considerable controversy, and it is not clear that they will be accepted.

The real problems in Mexican labor relations, though, stem less from the standards themselves than from the laxity of enforcement. Most Mexican workers are in the informal economy and are therefore not covered by any laws. Those without work have few protections. Even union members are not as well looked after as might be supposed because their leaders are more concerned with preserving their connection to the state/party than defending workers' interests. In reviewing Mexico's labor laws, Arturo Alcalde, a labor lawyer, said, "You're in a world of science fiction. The theory is different from the practice."[40]

Liberal groups in the three countries have proposed a "social charter," similar to the European Community's "Charter of Fundamental Social Rights for Workers."[41] The EC charter lists numerous goals, including collective bargaining, equal treatment for men and women, health and safety, and protection of children, the elderly, and the disabled. These rights would appear compatible with laws or norms in all three North American countries, nevertheless all three governments are nervous about adopting such a charter.

U.S. labor unions have proposed a charter because they fear that integration between two economies at such different levels of development will lead to the reduction of living standards, wages, and working conditions in the United States. To prevent that, they want to legislate specific thresholds in each of these areas. A study of the relationship between trade and labor standards worldwide suggests that increased trade can improve a country's labor standards, but this improvement does not occur immediately, and whether it occurs at all depends on the political framework in the particular country and the governing philosophy of its leaders.[42] Briefly, the neoclassical philosophy asserts that the best way to improve labor standards is not to interfere with the market by legislating higher wages or better working conditions. The neo-institutionalists, on the contrary, believe that the best way to sustain development is to increase aggregate demand by legislating an improvement in wages and working conditions. The empirical evidence suggests that both arguments might be true: low wages and an easygoing regulatory climate are apparently necessary to attract investment and promote early growth in poorer areas, but unless wages rise after a certain period, further development is inhibited.

Jerome Levinson has argued that a social charter and improvements in Mexican labor standards are infeasible as long as unions are subordinate to the Mexican state, while the state pursues an economic strategy designed to promote foreign investment by holding wages down.[43] There are other structural reasons why wages and working conditions might not improve in Mexico as fast as the neoclassical theory would suggest. Despite more investment, wages might stagnate because of the large numbers of unemployed and underemployed among Mexico's expanding population. With lower trade barriers in effect, foreign investors are likely to import new technology, which is rarely labor-intensive. Finally, depending on how Mexican subsistence agriculture adapts to NAFTA and the government's new agrarian reform program, a medium-to-large exodus from the rural to the urban areas of Mexico can be expected. These structural impediments might preclude a rise in labor standards for several years.

The idea of linking social improvements abroad with U.S. trade policy is not new. The Smoot-Hawley Tariff of 1930 included a set of social policies as preconditions for trading, and some provisions, such as prohibiting imports made by prison labor, remain law. In the past two decades, the U.S. Congress has conditioned trade benefits, like the generalized system of tariff preferences, and investment guarantees on whether a foreign government protects the basic rights of its workers. The Omnibus Trade and Competitiveness Act of 1988 makes violation of labor rights an "unfair trade practice." Most recently, the U.S. government signed an agreement with the Peoples Republic of China on August 7, 1992, that will permit U.S. diplomats to inspect Chinese institutions to see whether they are exporting products made with prison labor.[44] Although there are numerous precedents, some sixty years old, for the United States to insist on at least minimally decent social conditions abroad as a prerequisite for trade, NAFTA specifies none of these conditions.

HUMAN RIGHTS AND DEMOCRACY

The governments of Spain, Portugal, and Greece understood that the price of entry into the Common Market was democracy and respect for human rights. That served as a powerful incentive for the countries to become democratic and as a compelling deterrent against a military attempt to return to the old order. Many in the United States believe the same rule should apply to Mexico. As Congressman Robert Torricelli (D.-N.J.) put it bluntly, NAFTA "must be a democracies only club."[45] But Mexico has major problems conducting elections that are viewed as fair by opposition parties and the general public. It also continues to suffer serious, systemic human rights problems. The country's National Commission on Human Rights has begun an effective campaign to document cases and to try to remedy them, but the size of the problem exceeds the commission's grasp.

There are both moral and practical reasons why these political issues ought to concern the United States. Morally, as Senator Daniel P. Moynihan (D.-N.Y.) and Representative Torricelli imply, an agreement as intimate as NAFTA ought to be reserved for governments that share democratic values. From a practical standpoint, the U.S. government is likely to face both domestic political complaints and problems of enforcement in dealing with a country in which the rule of law is not the general rule. For example, from August through November 1992, three U.S. citizens died under suspicious circumstances either in or just after being released from Mexican jails. Their families lobbied Congress, and Representative Howard Berman, a Democrat from California, said he would raise the issue as NAFTA was being debated: "I support free trade and a closer relationship with Mexico. But it only works if there is a commitment to shared values of due process under law."[46]

Mexico also has human rights concerns vis-a-vis the United States. The treatment by U.S. border officials of undocumented Mexican workers has been criticized by the same international human rights groups that have censured Mexico. President George Bush's acquiescence in the kidnapping by the Drug Enforcement Agency of a Mexican citizen in Mexico, Dr. Humberto Alvarez Machain, in order to bring him to trial in the United States (on charges that he was involved in the torture and killing of a D.E.A. agent) was roundly and justifiably condemned by the international community, and the government's case was so weak that a federal judge threw it out and permitted Dr. Alvarez to return to Mexico. Bush made matters worse by asserting as principle the right of the United States to kidnap foreigners in their countries. To the extent that the United States presses its concerns about human rights, one can be sure that Mexico will raise these countervailing issues as well. In that sense, NAFTA will be a vehicle for a wider, two-sided political agenda.

A perplexing puzzle for U.S. policymakers is how to relate NAFTA to these political concerns. *Is Mexico more likely to complete its journey to democracy and rule of law if that is a precondition for membership to NAFTA, or is entry into NAFTA more likely to increase the prospects of a successful democratic transition?* It is worth recalling that Mexico was one of the few countries in Latin America that rejected the Alliance for Progress, and the reason was its unwillingness to accept U.S. preconditions.

When, as late as 1978, a governor of a northern Mexican state mentioned to Mexican president Jose López Portillo that it might be useful to request some aid from the United States to rehabilitate a border town, López Portillo angrily replied, "Do not tell me that, not even as a joke." Mexico's newspapers reported that the governor was compelled to "publicly apologize to López Portillo for considering the possibility of U.S. aid."[47] Much has changed since then, but what has not is Mexican rejection of American conditions of a political nature.

Because of Mexican sensitivities, the best way for the United States to achieve a political objective in Mexico is rarely the shortest distance between two points. The issue of Mexican political practices has to be handled very delicately by the U.S. government, lest it evoke the opposite of what is intended. An indirect strategy that includes international election observers might be helpful to deal with the endemic problems of the presence of coercion and a lack of popular confidence in the political system. Similarly, private groups, not prescriptions from the U.S. government, probably offer the most constructive advice for influencing Mexico's political behavior. Human rights groups, universities, labor unions, and businessmen can and should play a role, preferably in conjunction with their Mexican counterparts, to increase respect for human rights.

In the long term, in my judgment, the logic of twin liberalizations will be compelling: if the economic walls come down between the United States and Mexico, the political walls within Mexico cannot stand. To impose a democratic precondition on Mexico—insisting on democracy before NAFTA is ratified—would be shortsighted and counterproductive. NAFTA will be more of an asset than a liability in opening up the Mexican political system simply because it will increase the integration of Mexican society with those of its liberal, democratic neighbors to the north.

CHAPTER 5

THE CLINTON PROPOSAL AND
RELATED OPTIONS:
A WIDER, DEEPER NAFTA

W hat NAFTA lacks is a vision of the national interest and a strategy for achieving that. The agreement is based on the assumption that elimination of all barriers to trade and investment will create a market with magical qualities that will benefit all. NAFTA's opponents argue that the "invisible hand" of the marketplace often has negative consequences for certain strata of the population and cannot deal adequately with collective problems like the environment. Their concerns are neither paranoid nor irrational; they are based on the understanding that the world is changing very rapidly and that the gains from those changes are being distributed unequally.

On the other hand, rejection of NAFTA would sap Mexico's confidence, undermining its well-being and perhaps imperiling its new economic program. The Mexican government took a serious risk in opening itself up to a closer relationship with the United States; if Washington rejected NAFTA, it would strengthen those who have long insisted that Americans cannot be trusted. Even so, the United States should not accept NAFTA just to respond affirmatively to Mexican risk taking. Better reasons are that the agreement is in our interest, that our future requires adaptation to new challenges, and that the two countries can help each other acquire a global competitive edge.

What is needed is a long-term strategy that meshes an expanded view of what NAFTA can achieve with effective policy responses to many of the issues raised by its opponents. Such an approach should not maintain trade and investment barriers; nor should it interfere with the market. Rather, it should correct or compensate for the market's dysfunctions and inequities.

On October 4th, 1992, in the heat of a presidential campaign, Democratic candidate Bill Clinton went to North Carolina State University to announce his support for the North American Free Trade Agreement and to explain his decision: "If it is done right, it will create jobs in the United States and in Mexico, and if it is done right, and it is part of a larger economic strategy, we can raise our incomes and reverse the awful trend of now more than a decade in which most Americans are working harder for less money."

The central issue, in his mind, was "how we can compete and win in the global economy." He explained the changes that had occurred in the United States and the world in the previous generation--growing dependence on trade, intensifying economic competition, increasing mobility of money and production. The United States lost high-wage jobs and a significant part of its manufacturing base, but Germany and Japan did not. In the United States, 16.5 percent of the work force is in manufacturing as compared to 28 percent in Japan and 32 percent in Germany. In Clinton's view, success in other countries was owed to better training, more investment in modern plant and equipment, greater spending on nonmilitary research and development, more cooperation between business, government, and labor, and lastly, protection of high-wage jobs. He pointed out that only 16 percent of the European automobile market is open to foreigners, and only 3 percent of all the cars in Japan are not of Japanese make. "The issue," he concluded, "is not whether we should support free trade or open markets. Of course, we should. The real issue is whether or not we will have a national economic strategy to make sure we reap the benefits."

His arguments for NAFTA were many, but in brief he asserted, "We need stronger ties to our neighbors both for positive opportunities and to protect us in the event that other countries become more protectionist." NAFTA can help create U.S. jobs, but it is less important than other domestic economic policies, and its success depends on the way in which it is implemented. Clinton proposed five items to be included in the implementing legislation that the United States can take care of unilaterally, without requiring negotiation, and three supplemental agreements to be negotiated with Canada and Mexico, saying, "I will not sign legislation implementing the North American Free Trade Agreements until we have reached additional agreements to protect America's vital interests."

The five unilateral steps are: (1) adjustment assistance, education, and training for vulnerable workers and communities; (2) better protection of the environment; (3) help for agriculture, by applying American pesticide requirements to imported food and by offering aid for affected farmers to grow alternative crops; (4) opening the dispute-settlement process to citizen challenges regarding the environment and workers' standards; and (5) ensuring that temporary professional immigrants not be permitted to break strikes.

Most of these issues can be dealt with readily in the implementing legislation and do not need a detailed analysis here. The most important item is the first. In his May 1, 1991, letter to Congress, President Bush assured legislators that he was committed to a worker adjustment program that included retraining, but in his previous three budgets he had eliminated this program that had originated in the 1962 Trade Act. Jobs and retraining became pivotal issues in the campaign, and Clinton promised a comprehensive package of adjustment assistance that included funding for training, health care, income support, and assistance for communities adversely affected by trade. Bush finally responded with his own plan, New Century Workforce, on August 24, 1992, two weeks after the announcement of NAFTA, and the Clinton campaign acknowledged that its program had influenced Bush's.[1]

Instead of comparing the programs, it would be better to identify some of the issues that need to be resolved in assembling a trade adjustment package. The problem in deciding whether to give adjustment assistance is that it is often very difficult to identify one overriding reason why a firm shuts down. In 1991, 87,592 businesses failed in this country, and unemployment was about 8.5 million.[2] There were many reasons why these firms failed—bad management, low demand because of local, regional, or national recession, high interest rates, poor-quality product, competition from firms across the street, in the next state, or abroad, an absentee or low-quality labor force, inability to market or advertise well, lack of innovation or use of new technology. Import competition may or may not figure as one of the causes of business failure. Who is to determine, and how can one determine, instances in which fair or unfair import competition is an important cause of business failure? Even if one could identify trade as the cause of failure, should that enterprise, that worker, or that community have a greater right to aid than those that saw their economic activity melt away because of a reduction in defense spending, more stringent environmental regulations, or just plain bad luck?

The Bush administration answered these questions with a five-year, $10 billion New Century Workforce program for retraining and transition assistance for workers who lose their jobs or are "vulnerable to displacement," *regardless of the cause*. This might make sense economically, but it does not deal with the political logic of the free trade debate. The original trade adjustment assistance package was developed by Congress during its debate on the Trade Expansion Act of 1962; it was partly a political device to keep the freer trade coalition together, and to demonstrate that the government wanted to help those who would be injured by trade. The Labor Advisory Committee's criticism of Bush for scrapping the Trade Adjustment Assistance (TAA) program is a sign that a vulnerable group felt that the program helped. Labor recommended strengthening the program to include a two-year training program, medical insurance coverage, "bridge benefits" for those near retirement, targeted job creation, and job search and relocation allowances.[3]

It is difficult to estimate the necessary size of such a program. Nevertheless, based on their initial estimate that 112,000 workers will be displaced by NAFTA and that each worker would receive $8,000 (based on current expenditures), Gary C. Hufbauer and Jeffrey J. Schott recommend an appropriation of $900 million for such assistance.[4] The Bush administration's proposed $2 billion per year was for all dislocations, which it estimated would add up to about 400,000 people. The amount of adjustment assistance in either case is still trivial compared to the annual increase in the value of U.S. exports and foreign investment flows to Mexico.

The question of how to discourage firms from relocating to Mexico is similarly vexing. Could those firms that chose to move part or all of their facilities to Mexico have remained solvent if they stayed in the United States? If U.S. firms do not go to Mexico, would they simply go to another country—in Southeast Asia or Eastern Europe—that imports less from the United States than does Mexico? Because one of the explicit purposes of NAFTA is to encourage foreign investment in Mexico, it is completely unsurprising that the agreement does not approach such questions from the perspective of trying to restrict the flow of capital. Clinton did not suggest precluding such investment, but he did argue for elimination of the provisions in the tax code that provide incentives for relocation.

By reducing internal and external barriers to trade and investment, NAFTA will permit U.S. companies to think continentally as they calculate their costs of production and seek new markets both within the three countries and outside. This is likely to improve the efficiency of production, allowing for better merchandise at lower prices. Some U.S. businesses will no doubt conclude that they should close shop and move to Mexico in order to be able to compete. Other firms will face a more difficult choice whether to move or to invest in new technology to remain competitive.

The U.S. government has the responsibility to try to influence that choice by using two-tiered tax and credit incentives. First, for those businesses that relocate, the government needs to provide retraining and adjustment assistance to the workers left behind. Part of the cost of retraining should be defrayed by the departing companies themselves. Washington should also compel those firms to provide prior notification of their intention to leave. Second, firms in industries deemed adversely affected by the free trade agreement should be encouraged through tax deductions or credits to remain. The government should provide roughly the same level of retraining assistance for workers in firms staying put, while they make needed adjustments to the new environment, as for workers in departing firms.

Clinton also called for three supplemental agreements with Mexico and Canada—to establish commissions on the environment and on workers' standards and to deal with unanticipated changes in the flow of trade. The commissions that he envisages would have "substantial powers and resources," but it appears that their function would not include enforcement of the agreement; nor would they compel each member state to honor its own laws. They would use a variety of instruments—especially publicity and moral pressure—to encourage each government to promote collective norms and execute its own laws. Such bodies, then, would be intermediate in the scope of their powers, lying between binational groups that collect information and occasionally monitor problems—like the North American Commission on Environmental Cooperation established by the Bush and Salinas administrations in September 1992—and multinational commissions that collectively enforce treaties, such as the EC Commission.

While it might be desirable to move toward collective enforcement, and while some in the United States might want to play a more direct role enforcing Mexico's environmental laws or health and safety standards, the Mexican government would not look on such a proposal kindly. Instead of rejecting outright a U.S. request to participate in enforcement of Mexican laws, however, Mexico would be cleverer to insist on reciprocity. That would probably squelch the idea because the U.S. government is just as nationalistic, if not more so, about defending its "sovereignty" against international groups or committees trying to enforce universal norms within the United States. Indeed, the Labor Advisory Committee vehemently condemned the dispute-settlement provisions in NAFTA for weakening U.S. sovereignty by giving arbitration panels the right to decide on trade complaints.

Mexican president Salinas indicated that he is prepared to talk about these commissions and other ideas proposed by Clinton, but he suggested indirectly that if Clinton were to begin such negotiations, he might also introduce some proposals of his own, for example, on immigration and on support for building up Mexico's infrastructure.[5] The Canadian prime minister has not yet responded to Clinton's ideas, but since they are directed more at the U.S.-Mexican relationship, any hesitation on the part of Canada should have little effect on either NAFTA or the supplemental agreements.

In negotiating the forms these commissions take, the three governments should begin by seeking a statement of norms and standards. In the environmental area, most issues are relatively clear-cut, nonetheless a good analysis needs to be done concerning the discrepancies between laws on environmental protection in the United States, Canada, and Mexico. Negotiators of the three governments need to discuss these differences and make recommendations on ways each law should be modified in order to reach common and higher standards. The publicity generated by such a commission could help in educating people throughout North America on these issues.

After agreeing to norms and standards, the next step would be for the commission to develop a capacity to monitor the environment and investigate problems. To be effective, the commission and its staff would need to be semiautonomous—that is to say, they would be appointed by the three governments, but they would not be government officials. They could be chosen from environmental groups, the business world, or elsewhere.

Clinton's proposal also calls for giving the environmental commission resources for education and training, for serving as a forum for citizen complaints, and for dealing with new issues, such as process standards for resource extraction or manufacturing.[6] It is not clear how this commission would stop pollution or prescribe remedies except perhaps by moral suasion or the public attention it brings to such issues. In the long term, however, depending on how the commission works, the three countries might contemplate transferring some enforcement authority to it.

Clinton's Commission for Workers' Standards and Safety would have similar powers to train, educate, develop minimum standards, and resolve disputes. Its purpose, again, would be to open the decisionmaking process to public citizens, while relying on each country to enforce its own standards. Of course, if the three countries can agree on a single set of standards, then the step toward joint investigation and enforcement is not such a large one. Given the difference in labor-government relations in the three countries and the asymmetry in levels of economic development, though, it could be difficult to negotiate a single set of labor standards. A report of the Office of Technology Assessment suggests a modest outline for such a "social charter": the right to a stable job that pays above-poverty rates; the right to training and education throughout working life; the right to organize and bargain collectively; and limiting income inequality.[7]

The problem with such a charter is that the rights are empty unless governments assume responsibility to enforce them, and however desirable a full-employment economy might be, the fiscal costs of mandating it are almost certainly beyond what the U.S. Congress is prepared to contemplate at this time. Therefore, the fundamental choice in legislating such a charter is either to adopt the Mexican-European style of declaring unrealistic or infeasible goals or to incorporate into the charter only those laws that can and should be enforced. A charter that limits itself to defining a more modest set of standards shared by the three governments would constitute a good first step toward defending workers' rights on the continent. Those standards could include: the right to bargain collectively, child labor laws, an antidiscrimination clause, and the right to a "healthy working environment" with explicit minimum conditions guaranteed. The very act of negotiating these topics would raise the level of attention given them. These rights should have already been negotiated and included in NAFTA; it is an unfortunate signal to working people that the three governments spent more time focusing on intellectual property rights than on workers' rights.

There is much else that a health and labor standards commission can and should do.[8] It needs to establish binational groups to collect better data on the levels of exposure to hazards in the workplace and the environment. It could start with routine measurements of the water and air quality at the border. It could undertake a comprehensive surveillance of health conditions on both sides of the border. Only after doing such studies would the commission be able to decide on the priority problems that need to be attacked.

The commission should build up the capacity of Mexico to handle problems related to occupational safety. The government of Mexico cannot improve conditions until it has trained inspectors, industrial hygienists, and occupational health people (including doctors) who know how to handle the needs of an industrial area. The U.S. Department of Labor and the Occupational Safety and Health Administration could help in training these people and providing them equipment. After the Mexicans have developed their inspectorate personnel, it might be easier to discuss harmonizing standards and to encourage collaborative research and exchange programs on workplace safety.

The commission should undertake a thorough review of occupational safety conditions and the capacity to enforce standards in each country. Based on that study, the commission should develop operational goals and timetables for reaching those goals. It could also help establish on a pilot basis joint labor-management health and safety committees in industrial sites. Each committee would be trained to prepare an analysis and a work plan. Much of this work could be facilitated by non-governmental groups, like the Mexico-U.S. Committee on Occupational and Environmental Health, chaired by Dr. Howard Frumkin and Dr. Maricio Hernandez, and the National Safe Workplace Institute, based in Chicago.[9]

The AFL-CIO recommends that the United States go a step further, by negotiating provisions whereby a country imposes trade sanctions against another that violates labor rights or workplace standards. The sanctions could involve a partial or total removal of duty-free status, a prohibition on the importation of a particular product, or simply a warning. It would be desirable for such a judgment to be made by the Trade Commission within the context of its dispute-settlement mechanism, after a finding by the health and safety commission.

On the border area, the environmental commission and the occupational standards commission could work together, by setting emission standards for the border area, by inspecting businesses and imposing fines, and by using the ensuing funds to finance their operations and to clean up toxic wastes. The two commissions could jointly review the implementation, enforcement, and compliance with the laws and the treaties in the area of the environment and on the social agenda each year.[10]

The third supplemental agreement proposed by Clinton is somewhat vague. He calls for action to deal with an "unexpected surge in imports." Existing U.S. trade laws and NAFTA have provisions for such cases where a rapid increase in imports would seriously injure a particular industry. Perhaps an addendum could be spelled out that would permit some identifiable action when both the GATT and NAFTA prove inadequate. Naturally, such an addendum would need to be defined with some precision, or else it would risk reopening the entire agreement. After all, both Canada and Mexico first approached the United States for a free trade agreement in order to preclude arbitrary action against their exports.

It might be more useful to consider Clinton's proposal in the wider context of helping all three countries address the unforeseen problems that will arise as the growth in trade and deepening integration begin to complicate their relations. NAFTA will lead to more disagreements, not fewer, because as trade increases, more businesses and workers will become dependent on the success or the failure of doing business internationally. The U.S.-Canada agreement has been in effect since 1989. By 1992, 66 percent of the Canadian public opposed the agreement, and only 6 percent believed that Canada had gained from it. Canadians believe that there have been more trade disputes since the agreement came into force, that these are getting more contentious and difficult to resolve, and that Canada is losing most of the battles.[11]

More systematic studies of the effect of the agreement on Canada's economy suggest the opposite—that Canadian industry has become more competitive and that the agreement has stimulated growth in Canada, although insufficient growth to overcome the country's recession.[12] Similarly, experts have analyzed the dispute-settlement mechanism in the U.S.-Canadian agreement and have concluded that it is not only fair, but a model for what GATT should adopt.[13] The public mood, however, is more influential than the experts' views in determining whether the agreement will be maintained, let alone expanded.

Given this pattern, one can expect that the visible benefits of NAFTA will not measure up to the Bush administration's advertisements, that most dislocations or plant closings will be blamed on NAFTA, that North American trade disputes will seem to increase in number and intensity, that most people will ignore the growth in trade or attribute it to something other than NAFTA, and the opponents of NAFTA will use these cases as proof that they were right. To cope with this awkward transition while trying to build confidence in the agreement, the North American governments should anticipate the kinds of controversies that are likely to arise and counter them by developing new procedures and institutions to maintain and improve the agreement.

First, the three governments should adopt a "double-standard test." Before telling another government how to manage its affairs, a leader needs to think about how he or she would feel hearing a similar message. Anthony Solomon, who was president of the Federal Reserve Bank in New York, recalls a lecture by Secretary of State George Shultz to Latin American foreign ministers about the dangers of excessive deficit financing. "I couldn't resist," Solomon recalls, "asking Shultz in an innocent voice when he returned to our table if he might have been referring to his own country."[14] President Bush failed the test when he asserted a right to kidnap foreign nationals in their home country, as in the case of Humberto Alvarez Macháin. Perhaps if he had stopped to ask himself how the American people would have reacted if Mexico had kidnapped an American from Chicago, he would have acted differently.

The president needs to take the lead to alert the nation to the diplomatic dangers of lecturing a foreign government, especially when many complex problems carry enough blame for both sides. Newspaper editors and others from throughout the country might then pick up the baton and remind people that corruption is found not only in Mexico or that Canada is not the only nation in the area with worries about its cultural identity, and that these and other matters are of legitimate concern to our neighbors as well as to us.

The three governments need to develop "early warning systems" to alert decisionmakers to approaching problems. No one wants to wait for a small problem that could be resolved by negotiations to be converted into a "sovereignty" issue. To the extent that both sides can identify such problems early, the prospects of resolving them are greater.

The future agenda will be filled with potential disputes because in a free trade area, any domestic policy that confers a discriminatory advantage on a country's exports or a disadvantage on imports is legitimately a trade issue, and any selective tax incentive that affects a firm's relocation is an investment issue. Once tariffs and quotas are drained away, islands of trade-related "distortions" emerge and become the most visible features of the new landscape. If a country's laws require that imports be produced according to certain safety, labor, or environmental standards, then a nontrade item becomes a trade issue. Also eligible for negotiation in the new free trade era are policies like sales taxes, subsidized oil or gas prices, tax inducements, access to timber on government lands at below-market prices, and so on. Labor rights or worker compensation in one country becomes an issue in the others. As integration proceeds, the line that separates internal and external issues blurs.

These new issues of interdependence will probably involve what Michael Hart describes as "sensitive domestic regulatory schemes." These include most domestic policies—income- and price-support programs, communications and cultural issues, competition or antitrust policy, health care, environmental and production standards, among others. As Hart put it, these issues differ from those on the traditional trade agenda. They "do not involve concession swapping but rule writing. To a much greater extent, they engage concerns about national sovereignty."[15] In practice, they will require extensive consultations and negotiations to harmonize domestic policies. NAFTA has placed all three governments on this road. As the example of the European Community has shown, it is a long and hazardous one.

To staff the "early warning systems," to seek out opportunities for cross-border collaboration, and to discuss and formulate approaches to the harmonization of national policies, new North American institutions will be necessary. The Trade Commission is a useful start, but it is obviously inadequate to the range and magnitude of the task. The Clinton proposal to establish independent commissions on the environment and workers' standards is also a good step, but instead of having a multitude of independent commissions, it would be preferable to have an umbrella North American Commission with offices to deal with trade disputes, the environment, workers' rights, human rights, border development, and, not the least important, the collection and harmonization of statistics. In particular, the Commission could help Mexico to upgrade its statistical capabilities,[16] and it could encourage the United States to move more rapidly to a metric system. The Commission should be structured in such a way that it can foster constructive dialogue between the three governments on subjects from the routine to the controversial, like immigration.

The immigration issue is particularly difficult because of the profound ambivalence that most Mexicans and Americans feel toward the subject. Most Mexicans would prefer more labor mobility between the two countries, and some see emigration as an "escape valve" to release pressures that could, if bottled up in Mexico, create social tensions or political instability. At the same time, Mexicans are embarrassed that their people have to leave the country in order to make a living. Most Americans would prefer fewer immigrants, but their opinions are often contradictory. Liberals feel split between their desire to welcome the poor from abroad and uneasiness that the immigrants' progress might be at the expense of blacks and other people at the bottom of the economic ladder. Conservatives are torn between their preference for a free market, particularly cheaper labor, and a wariness that more immigration could dilute the prevailing culture and divide the nation. These conflicting emotions would make negotiations more convoluted.

Still, there is much to discuss. The Mexican government wants the United States to increase its immigration quotas and treat undocumented workers more humanely. The U.S. government would like Mexican cooperation to deal with smugglers of undocumented workers. The United States also needs to make some difficult decisions concerning the overall level of immigration. The 1990 Immigration Act raised legal immigration by about 40 percent at a time when public sentiment, including that of Mexican-Americans, is moving in the opposite direction.[17] Seventy-five percent of Mexican-American citizens and 84 percent of Mexican resident aliens in the United States believe that immigration is already too high.[18] This could signify that everyone— especially relative newcomers—might like a pause in the influx in order to assimilate and advance without the relentless competition of new immigrants willing to work for less. One of the reasons that statistics on Hispanics in the United States indicate they suffer lower levels of education and health is that the constant flow of new immigrants drags the averages down. These statistics should not be taken to imply that the newest wave is not assimilating or progressing. An analysis of generational change among Hispanic immigrants suggests the same pattern of advancement and integration as with previous waves,[19] such as turn-of-the-century immigrants whose progress only became evident two decades after their immigration was halted by a new law. Current immigration to the United States should not be ended but a legitimate question is whether some temporary and small reduction might not be desirable. This issue should be discussed both within the country and between the United States and Mexico.

Like trade, immigration benefits both nations, but it has serious distributional consequences that are rarely considered. In the sending countries, it often creates "welfare" communities that rely on remittances from abroad rather than their own local production. In the receiving nations, the upper classes benefit from the availability of cheaper labor, but the working classes often suffer from the increased competition. This problem is exacerbated when the immigration is illegal and thus more easily exploited by businesses.

Many other issues need to be reviewed. The United States and Mexico have cooperated in trying to stop illegal drug trafficking but have achieved little success. New ways need to be found to deal with the growing inequalities that arise out of integration. Salinas's "Solidarity Program" aimed at empowering communities ought to be examined as a possible model, along with American local initiatives like The Atlanta Project and Rebuild L.A.

An example of how the progress of integration could either become a source of dispute or an opportunity to improve on existing public policy comes in the area of health care. Americans know that their public health-care system is in need of fundamental change. Some feel that they would profit from looking at the Canadian system. At the same time, however, Canadians are worried that the high cost of their health care might cause their businesses to move south with the advent of free trade. They are disturbed as well that the low prices of prescription drugs available to them might soar as a result of the patents agreement in NAFTA. Americans find that in Mexico health care and drugs are so inexpensive that it pays for them to cross the border routinely.[20] All of this suggests the North American governments would do well to discuss what they can learn from each other in traditionally domestic policy fields like health care.

The presence of Canada at the negotiating table could help U.S.-Mexican relations, since Canada shares with Mexico the perspective of the more vulnerable neighbor and shares with the United States a democratic history and a similar culture. Instead of viewing each country's concerns as a potential problem, all should borrow from each other to yield the best overall result. The United States has concerns about human rights in Mexico. Mexico has parallel concerns about the treatment by the United States of Mexicans. Canadians are fearful that they cannot keep out the guns so readily available in the United States. Would it not be desirable for each government to reinforce positive trends—respecting human rights and restricting guns—in concert with its neighbors?

Mexico is reluctant to consider supranational institutions for fear that the United States could control them, but the truth is that

Washington is stronger in dealing with problems on a case-by-case basis than if it had to submit to a genuinely trinational forum that employed agreed-on principles and resolved disputes based on a neutral set of rules. Such a forum is essential to sustain confidence in all three countries that disputes will be settled fairly. The North American Commission would not be a panacea, but rather a device to anticipate, contain, and hopefully resolve the new problems posed by growing interdependence.

LESSONS FROM EUROPE. The trauma of two world wars that ravaged the Continent in the twentieth century finally induced Europeans to contemplate new forms of supranational cooperation, the most important of which was the European Economic Community, set up in 1957 following the Treaty of Rome. From the beginning, the European governments designed institutions to discuss common problems (the European Parliament) and to implement policy (the European Commission).

The European Community also developed regional policies to help poorer areas like Italy's Mezzogiorno take advantage of the opportunities of freer trade, and to help declining areas of richer countries adjust to the dislocations of freer trade. A Common Agricultural Policy endeavored to stabilize farmers' incomes; the European Investment Bank (EIB) made loans, some of them interest-free, for regional development; and the European Social Fund (ESF) provided aid for education and retraining. In 1975, two years after the Community expanded to take in the United Kingdom, Denmark, and Ireland, the European Regional Development Fund (ERDF) was established as a formal mechanism to provide aid to remote and economically stagnant areas.[21]

Europe's experience in upgrading its poorer areas contains some lessons of possible relevance to NAFTA. Portugal, the poor man of Europe, was an original member of the European Free Trade Association (EFTA), established in 1960. Its per capita income was about 20 percent of those of its Scandinavian associates, and its wage levels were even lower, but Joseph McKinney, an economist from Baylor University, found "no evidence of a massive migration of industries from other EFTA countries to Portugal. Neither was there apparent downward pressure upon wages or increased unemployment in the other EFTA countries."[22]

Spain's entry into the European Community in 1986 is more pertinent as a forerunner of Mexico's integration into NAFTA than Portugal's experience in EFTA, even though the EC, unlike NAFTA, is a common market with free movement of labor as well as goods and services. Both Portugal and Spain had authoritarian political systems and highly regulated, protected economies, but Portugal was much poorer and did not change its economic strategy until decades *after* it entered EFTA. Spain was better prepared than Portugal for entry into the EC, having, like Mexico today, reduced its trade barriers, liberalized its investment rules, and deregulated its economy.

Many in Spain feared increased competition if they joined the European Community, and many in the EC worried that firms would move south to take advantage of Spain's cheaper labor, but it later became apparent that the positive effects on Spain of access to the European market had been underestimated while the negative effects on the EC had been overestimated. "Since this country joined the European Community in 1986," wrote Alan Riding of *The New York Times*, "huge dollops of capital from abroad have swiftly transformed it from a forgotten economic backwater into a new land of opportunity." This, he noted, is because grants from the EC amounted to roughly 3 percent of Spain's gross domestic product, more than matching the amount of foreign investment in the country.[23]

Significantly, Spain's development did not come at the expense of the rest of Europe. This was partly due to the well-developed job security arrangements in the EC, embodied in the social charter covering workers' rights, but also because of adjustment assistance in the north and development aid in the south of Europe. As Donald Puchala noted, "The institutions established to administer the Common Market have become rather formidable political forces in their own right."[24]

NAFTA negotiators showed little interest in learning from the EC experience. If the EC's recent political problems indicate that it may have over-institutionalized, NAFTA seems eager to make the opposite mistake, with only a single Trade Commission chartered and two other functionally specific groups on the drawing board. The European example, however, suggests that the three North American governments should consider introducing an institution with a broader mandate, a North American Council, and another to finance the integration process, perhaps a North American Bank for Development and Adjustment Assistance (NABDAA).[25]

The bank would have a dual purpose: to provide low-interest loans to Mexico for infrastructure and transportation development, and to furnish education and adjustment assistance to communities in the United States (and Canada) that are adversely affected by trade. This bank would be designed to be more flexible than the international development banks, and it could target communities rapidly for either development loans or adjustment grants. Adjustment assistance could just as easily be provided by a U.S. government agency, but the purpose of joining that task with a mission to facilitate the development of Mexico is to make a political statement in recognition that although trade is good for both countries, not everyone benefits. The Bank could be capitalized like the development banks. Each member country would make a paid-in contribution. The Bank could then borrow from the international markets. User fees could be collected on roads and bridges built in Mexico with Bank funds, and used to pay back the loans.

At this moment, when the United States is seeking ways to trim its deficit, the idea of a new North American development bank may strike some as unrealistic. But the point of having such a bank is to redirect our thinking as well as our resources to shaping the long-term effects of integration. President Salinas mentioned his interest in the idea in an interview on December 7, and after their meeting on January 8, Clinton noted that because of the disparities in development, "we have to look at some of the models of what has been done in other parts of the world to see how both sides can win" from free trade.[26]

Whether a new bank is established or not, the three governments should consult on ways to ensure that the World Bank and the Inter-American Bank lend generously to Mexico. From its very beginnings until the end of 1991, the World Bank made 131 loans to Mexico for a total of $18.3 billion; the Inter-American Development Bank (IDB) made $6.2 billion in Mexican loans from its establishment through the same year. In 1991 alone, Mexico received eight loans from the World Bank valued at $2.1 billion and three loans from the IDB adding up to $650 million.[27] But the resident representative of the United Nations Development Program in Mexico, Frederic Lyons, announced on November 3, 1992, that "Mexico has ceased to be a priority country for foreign aid."[28] If a North American Bank is not feasible at this time, it would be an especially poor moment to reduce Mexico's access to these important banks. To the contrary, the United States, working with Mexico, ought to try to reorient aid flows to those areas of the Mexican economy that have either the greatest opportunity to take advantage of NAFTA or the most serious potential problems.

REORGANIZING THE GOVERNMENT. NAFTA is a radical idea that does not fit comfortably into the current structure of the U.S. government. A new coordinating focus for pan-North American issues needs to be developed in both the executive and the legislative branches. The last time Washington considered this issue was when President Jimmy Carter appointed a coordinator of U.S.-Mexican Relations in 1979. The Reagan administration eliminated the office. Given the complexity of NAFTA, the diversity of the issues involved, and the increasing importance of relations with Canada and Mexico, the U.S. government ought to consider several options.

Within the State Department, the Office of Canadian Affairs is in the European bureau and Mexico is in the Latin American bureau. They need to be brought under the same roof. The State Department should consider appointing an undersecretary of state for North American affairs. The person should be of sufficient stature to deal directly with cabinet secretaries with jurisdiction over parts of the complicated relationship, and should be the president's coordinator for managing all of the different agencies in the U.S. government with responsibilities for intracontinental relations. That person will need a counterpart in at least one of the White House policy councils (National Security Council or Economic Council), preferably a deputy or perhaps a senior staff member. Either the under secretary of state or the policy council liaison should chair interagency meetings at the deputy cabinet level to ensure that policy toward Canada and Mexico is internally consistent.

A more modest approach would be to relocate Canadian affairs to the Bureau of Inter-American Affairs, and to appoint a deputy assistant secretary with responsibility for North American affairs. This would make sense because Canada has been playing an increasingly important role in Latin America and the Caribbean, beginning in the 1970s with an increase in aid to and trade with the region. In 1989 it joined the Organization of American States, and since then, Canadian representatives have played increasingly important roles in various hemispheric initiatives, including election monitoring in Nicaragua, Haiti, and Guyana.[29]

An intermediate option between an under secretary and a deputy assistant secretary would be to establish a new Bureau of North American Affairs and appoint an assistant secretary. Such a bureau would be staffed with officers from many of the agencies with responsibilities in Mexico.

Soon after NAFTA is ratified, a special planning unit should be established within the State Department's newly created Bureau of

North American Affairs to begin working with counterparts in Canada and Mexico. The new office should have three tasks: (1) to plan for the implementation of NAFTA and to begin to design the informal and formal intergovernmental mechanisms necessary to ensure a smooth transition with maximum public support; (2) to develop an agenda for the future and (3) to begin planning for the expansion of NAFTA to include the entire Western Hemisphere. Each task is large enough to fill the time of a major government department or rather important sections of virtually every government department. It is impractical to think that a single planning unit can accomplish these goals; what it needs to do is draft an outline of what is necessary and then delegate each task to a separate and larger intergovernmental group. With luck, all three tasks will be approached with the kind of energy and imagination that shaped the Marshall Plan. Without a new organizational base, however, these sweeping ideas have little chance of being translated into policies.

Congress ought to consider also ways to reorganize itself to provide ideas and direction for a new North American community. Perhaps the Joint Economic Committee, which does serious studies and is often led by some of the outstanding figures in Congress, could establish a special subcommittee on North American Affairs composed of leaders from the foreign affairs committees and the principal economic committees (Finance, Ways and Means) of both houses. This subcommittee, however, needs to do more than commission research and hold hearings; it should have some authority to consider legislation, and it should have some oversight capabilities.

CHAPTER 6

THE REGIONAL AND GLOBAL
IMPLICATIONS OF NAFTA

A major concern raised in regard to NAFTA is that it could have a deleterious effect on the General Agreement on Tariffs and Trade and on global free trade.[1] Neoclassical economic theory posits that a regional trading system is a "second-best solution" to free trade worldwide. Many economists believe that the proliferation of regional trading blocs will not only create significant trade-diversion effects (reducing overall trade), but they will undermine the global system. Jagdish Bhagwati, for example, has argued that the U.S. shift toward NAFTA could accelerate a break-up of the world trading system into blocs.[2] On a trip to Mexico City, Milton Friedman said that regional agreements such as NAFTA "are labeled free-trade agreements, but in point of fact, they are not. They would be more accurately described as managed-trade agreements." In his judgment, they are dangerous to free trade.[3]

These arguments are not without foundation, but there is evidence enough to argue that regional trading groups are more likely to be building blocks of than stumbling blocks to an improved world trading system. In the real world, the GATT is stagnating and seems unable to resolve the major issues on the trade agenda. A "breakthrough" on agricultural subsidies in November 1992, partially overcoming French objections, only revealed the large number of important issues— telecommunications, transportation, services, shipping, textiles—that have not yet been resolved. Moreover, the French obstruction of an agriculture agreement concealed other major obstacles, notably Japan's reluctance to end its ban on rice imports. The Uruguay Round, in short, is far from being completed, and whether the final text advances world interests in freer trade or not remains to be seen.

Long before NAFTA was even conceived, the world had been dividing up into regional trading *areas*. The most important is the European Community, but Japan's growing relationship with East Asia suggests the origins of a second powerful group. A brief comparison of these two areas and NAFTA is given in Table 6.1 (pages 90–91).

The most integrated of the three areas is the twelve-nation European Community, with a population of 345 million and a combined gross product of about $5.9 trillion in 1990. Responsible for 40 percent of all world trade, the EC, in Lawrence Krause's words, "is a huge exception to a non-discriminatory [international trade] regime."[4]

The EC has spent thirty-five years attempting to do what it promised in 1957—establish a Common Market. While trying to unify and deepen its internal market, it has had to cope with numerous other issues and problems. It needed to rework its relationship with its former colonies, the ACP (African, Caribbean, and Pacific) countries. The European Free Trade Association (EFTA) has agreed to a single unified free trade area with the EC starting January 1, 1993; several EFTA countries (Austria, Sweden, and Finland) have requested membership in the EC. Virtually every old and new nation in Eastern Europe has requested an association agreement with the EC; meanwhile, Germany, which had been providing most of the investment so desperately needed by countries of Eastern Europe and the former Soviet Union, is now concentrating its resources on integrating the former East Germany.

The global implication of these developments is that the EC has been looking inward. To advance toward its 1992 deadline, its members had to make internal political compromises at the expense of the region's international obligations. The EC's inability to achieve substantive reform of its Common Agricultural Policy, for example, effectively closed the European market to much of Latin American agricultural products and paralyzed the GATT trade negotiations for years.

Japan has become the economic center of an increasingly dynamic Asia, but aside from ASEAN, a trade grouping of six Southeast Asian nations, there is as yet no formal trade regime that could compare to the European Community. Most of the Asian nations are increasingly dependent on Japanese investment and the U.S. market. Lawrence

Krause proposes a "Pacific Basin" community that would include Japan, the United States, and thirteen other countries. According to him, the region's real trade growth in the 1980s was 8.7 percent—higher than the EC's 6 percent—and it was more integrated, with intraregional trade accounting for 65.7 percent of the total, as compared to 58.6 percent for the EC.[5] The idea merits consideration, but given the tremendous differences between the United States and Japan on trade policies and the continued difficulty that the United States and Latin America have in penetrating the Japanese and other Asian markets, a Pacific community seems much more distant than a Western Hemisphere economic area.

The North American trading area is already well developed. From the U.S. perspective, exports to Canada and Mexico have almost always exceeded exports to the European Community and Asia since 1955. (See Table 6.2, page 92.) In 1955, two years before the signing of the Treaty of Rome establishing the European Community, U.S. exports to Europe were valued at $2.6 billion, compared to $4 billion worth of exports to Canada and Mexico. Thirty-five years later, U.S. exports to Asia had increased much more rapidly than exports to Europe, but North America remained preeminent; U.S. exports to Canada and Mexico increased to $112 billion, or 28.4 percent of the total.

The trends are similar for U.S. imports, with North America accounting for one-quarter of them and Europe for 19 percent. The difference is the extraordinary growth of Japanese and Asian exports to the United States, from $1 billion in 1955 to nearly $100 billion in 1990, representing nearly 20 percent of total U.S. imports.

In analyzing the implications of NAFTA for the other two regional trading areas, it is useful to recall that all three areas have significant interests in the growth of world trade and in maintaining the GATT. This does not mean that they have equal interests. Though the United States is the first or second largest trader of goods in the world, Germany and Japan are much more dependent on world trade. More important, Japan and (to a lesser degree) Germany are more dependent on the U.S. market than the United States is on theirs (see Table 6.3, pages 94–5). Japan's exports to the United States represent roughly one-third of its total exports and about 3 percent of its GDP. In contrast, U.S. exports to Japan amount to about 11 percent of its total exports and less than 1 percent of GDP. Obviously, Japan has much more reason than the United States to fear getting locked out of its partner's market. Even though Germany is more dependent on the

TABLE 6.1
THE WORLD'S THREE MAIN TRADING AREAS: BASIC INDICATORS

REGION/COUNTRY	POPULATION (MILLIONS)		GNP (US$BILLIONS*)		GNP PER CAPITA* (US$*)		EXPORTS CUSTOMS BASIS, FOB (US$MILLIONS*)		IMPORTS CUSTOMS BASIS, CIF (US$MILLIONS*)	
	1970	1990	1970	1990	1970	1990	1970	1990	1970	1990
WESTERN HEMISPHERE	499.27	705.48	1,343.78	6,907.10	821.44	3,285.00	74,876	619,936	70,356	730,988
North America	278.59	362.70	1,225.96	6,204.60	3,339.27	14,916.67	60,610	523,236	56,664	659,580
United States	205.00	250.00	1,105.50	5,447.50	5,392.68	21,790.00	43,220	371,466	39,950	515,635
Canada	21.32	26.50	83.58	542.46	3,919.57	20,470.00	16,185	125,056	14,253	115,882
Mexico	52.27	86.20	36.88	214.64	705.57	2,490.00	1,205	26,714	2,461	28,063
Caribbean Basin	30.55	48.28	11.80	53.63	573.38	2,366.19	2,873	10,970	4,088	17,559
Central America	16.89	28.78	6.48	30.21	424.29	1,264.29	1,231	4,929	1,623	8,350
Caribbean	13.66	19.50	5.32	23.42	647.93	2,917.14	1,642	6,041	2,465	9,209
South America	190.13	294.50	106.02	648.87	587.0	1,725.00	11,393	85,730	9,604	53,849
Andean Pact	55.53	91.20	30.02	130.93	524.00	1,318.00	5,349	30,900	3,786	17,762
Mercosur	125.10	190.10	68.02	492.33	602.50	2,180.00	4,810	46,251	4,858	29,064
Chile	9.50	13.20	7.98	25.61	840.00	1,940.00	1,234	8,579	980	7,023

TABLE 6.1 (CONTINUED)

REGION/COUNTRY	POPULATION (MILLIONS)		GNP (US$BILLIONS*)		GNP PER CAPITA* (US$*)		EXPORTS CUSTOMS BASIS, FOB (US$MILLIONS*)		IMPORTS CUSTOMS BASIS, CIF (US$MILLIONS*)	
	1970	1990	1970	1990	1970	1990	1970	1990	1970	1990
EUROPEAN COMMUNITY	188.32	344.39	495.98	5,878.78	3,231.53	15,380.88	88,545	1,349,971	88,425	1,405,273
ASIA	346.16	512.32	242.12	3,772.56	444.90	7,742.22	31,812	641,969	35,819	674,477
Japan	104.00	123.50	203.30	3,140.61	1,954.81	25,430.00	19,320	286,768	18,880	231,223
ASEAN	204.21	316.77	29.88	300.71	353.83	3,240.00	6,161	140,537	7,696	160,369
Four Tigers	37.95	72.05	8.94	331.24	280.10	9,350.00	6,331	214,664	9,243	282,885

Key: Andean Pact : Peru, Colombia, Ecuador, Venezuela, Bolivia
Mercosur: Brazil, Argentina, Uruguay, Paraguay
European Community (1970): Belgium, France, Germany, Italy, Luxembourg, Netherlands
European Community (1990): Belgium, France, Germany, Italy, Luxembourg, Netherlands, Denmark, Greece, Ireland, Portugal, Spain, United Kingdom
ASEAN: Brunei, Malaysia, Singapore, Indonesia, Phillipines, Thailand
Four Tigers: Hong Kong, Singapore, South Korea, Taiwan

* Current
Notes: German 1990 population data after unification; German trade & GNP data are prior to unification; trade data for Belgium includes Luxembourg; and (*) Regional GNP per Capita are averages.
Sources: The World Bank, *World Tables*, 1984, 1991; and *World Development Report*, 1992; and U.S. Agency for International Development, *Latin American and Caribbean: Selected Economic and Social Data*, April 1992; and OECD *Monthly Statistics on Foreign Trade*, July 1992.

TABLE 6.2
U.S. EXPORTS TO NORTH AMERICA, EUROPE, AND ASIA (1945–1991)
(US$MILLIONS)

YEAR	CANADA & MEXICO	EC	JAPAN & SOUTHEAST ASIA	WORLD
1945	1,485	3,114	1,381	10,527
1955	3,969	2,614	2,144	15,518
1965	6,763	5,252	5,180	28,461
1975	26,885	22,865	19,658	109,317
1980	55,476	58,855	44,512	225,722
1985	66,922	45,776	51,036	213,146
1986	67,904	53,222	52,981	227,159
1987	74,396	60,629	58,244	254,122
1988	92,250	75,864	88,841	322,426
1989	103,791	86,424	101,509	363,812
1990	111,953	98,129	109,054	393,592
1991	118,379	103,209	109,674	421,614

Sources: U.S. Department of Commerce, International Trade Administration, *U.S. Foreign Trade Highlights*, 1992, 1988, 1985; U.S. Department of Commerce, Office of Business Economics, *U.S. Exports & Imports 1923–1968*, November 1970; U.S. Department of Commerce, Bureau of Economic Analysis, *U.S. Merchandise Trade: Exports & Imports, 1965–1976, 1977*; and U.S. Department of Commerce, Bureau of the Census, *Statistical Abstract of the United States*, various issues, 1950–1991.

United States than vice versa, the gap is much narrower, another reason why the European Community is less worried about NAFTA than it is about making its own rules and practices work. What this means is that NAFTA is likely to get the attention of Japan and Europe. Their first reaction may be negative and fearful, but realizing their stake in preserving the world system, they will concentrate their diplomatic energies on making GATT work. That will mean, among other things, using some of NAFTA's innovations—on agriculture, dispute settlement, treatment of services—to invigorate GATT.

HEMISPHERIC IMPLICATIONS

In the past, any Latin American initiative to seek closer relations with the United States provoked Mexican opposition. For a region seeking its identity in the shadow of a superpower, the Mexican objection often amounted to a veto. When Carlos Salinas changed the Mexican habit of rejecting the United States into a proposal for a free trade agreement, the rest of Latin America aroused itself to make an anxious entreaty to become part of the new economic club. Similar to Mexico, these countries were more fearful of being excluded than eager to become part of a larger community anchored by the United States. Their anxieties were not baseless. The trends in trade with the United States had been unfavorable and worsened demonstrably during the "lost decade" of the debt crisis. In 1955, nearly 20 percent of all U.S. imports came from South America; by 1990, that figure had declined to about 5 percent; the Caribbean suffered an equally dramatic decline, from 6.6 to 1.6 percent of U.S. imports. North American trade became more concentrated, to the point that since 1989, half of U.S. trade with Latin America has been with Mexico. If the rest of the region failed to secure access the U.S. market through treaty, it could be marginalized.

After several Latin American presidents requested the expansion of NAFTA to include their countries, President Bush responded on June 27, 1990, by opening the door to the possibility of a Western Hemisphere trade area. In his Enterprise for the Americas Initiative, Bush promised to negotiate free trade agreements with governments in the hemisphere that implemented market reforms. The U.S. government gave priority to NAFTA, but it advised interested Latin American governments to prepare for future talks by accelerating subregional integration schemes and negotiating "framework agreements" similar to the U.S.-Mexican one of 1987.

TABLE 6.3
TRADE DEPENDENCY OF THE THREE WORLD POWERS

UNITED STATES

	GDP @ MKT PRICES (US$MIL)	TOTAL EXPORTS (FOB) (US$MIL)	EXPORTS TO JAPAN (US$MIL)	% TOTAL U.S. EXPORTS (%)	EXPORTS TO JAPAN AS % OF US GDP (%)	EXPORTS TO GERMANY (US$MIL)	% TOTAL U.S. EXPORTS (%)	EXPORTS TO GERMANY AS % OF US GDP (%)
1960	509,000	20,600	1,341	6.51	0.26	1,068	5.18	0.21
1970	1,008,200	43,762	4,652	10.63	0.46	2,741	6.26	0.27
1980	2,684,400	225,722	20,790	9.21	0.77	10,960	4.86	0.41
1990	5,392,200	393,592	48,580	12.34	0.90	18,760	4.77	0.35
1991	5,672,600	421,600	48,147	11.42	0.85	21,317	5.06	0.38

JAPAN

	GDP @ MKT PRICES (US$MIL)	TOTAL EXPORTS (FOB) (US$MIL)	EXPORTS TO US (US$MIL)	% TOTAL JAPANESE EXPORTS (%)	EXPORTS TO US AS % OF JAPANESE GDP (%)	EXPORTS TO GERMANY (US$MIL)	% TOTAL JAPANESE EXPORTS (%)	EXPORTS TO GERMANY AS % OF JAPANESE GDP (%)
1960	50,095	4,709	1,149	24.40	2.29	372	7.90	0.74
1970	143,511	19,405	5,875	30.28	4.09	1,528	7.88	1.07
1980	1,840,335	130,441	30,867	23.66	1.68	5,786	4.44	0.31
1990	2,942,890	287,581	89,684	31.19	3.05	17,894	6.22	0.61
1991	3,642,975	338,329	91,583	27.07	2.51	20,631	6.10	0.57

TABLE 6.3 (CONTINUED)

GERMANY

	GDP @ MKT PRICES (US$MIL)	TOTAL EXPORTS (FOB) (US$MIL)	EXPORTS TO US (US$MIL)	% TOTAL GERMAN EXPORTS (%)	EXPORTS TO US AS % OF GERMAN GDP (%)	EXPORTS TO JAPAN (US$MIL)	% TOTAL GERMAN EXPORTS (%)	EXPORTS TO JAPAN AS % OF GERMAN GDP (%)
1960	84,481	15,394	897	5.83	1.06	88	0.57	0.10
1970	136,352	35,329	3,127	8.85	2.29	146	0.41	0.11
1980	775,667	192,861	11,924	6.18	1.54	2,186	1.13	0.28
1990	1,488,210	410,104	28,162	6.87	1.89	10,816	2.64	0.73
1991	1,728,152	439,135	26,229	5.97	1.52	10,745	2.45	0.62

Sources: World Bank, *World Development Report*, 1992; International Monetary Fund, *Direction of Trade Statistics*, 1976–1982, 1991, 1992; World Bank, *World Bank Tables*, 1976, 1988, 1991; U.S. Department of Commerce, International Trade Administration, *U.S. Foreign Trade Highlights*, 1992; U.S. Department of Commerce, Bureau of the Census, *Statistical Abstract of the United States*, various issues, 1950-1991; OECD, *Main Economic Indicators*, July 1992.

President Salinas pursued a similar approach with his neighbors. He offered the Central American governments a free trade agreement, sought and received associate membership in the Caribbean Community (CARICOM), and on July 20, 1991, he agreed with the presidents of Venezuela and Colombia to plan for a future three-way free trade zone.[6] Subsequently, he signed a free trade agreement with Chile.

Latin America embraced Bush's proposal and Salinas' example. Subregional trading groups—including old ones like the Andean Pact, the Central American Common Market, and the thirteen-nation CARICOM, and new ones like Mercosur (Argentina, Brazil, Uruguay, and Paraguay)—made more progress in lowering their internal trade barriers since 1990 than they had for decades. Virtually every nation negotiated a "framework" agreement with the United States as a basis for consulting on trade problems.[7]

The most surprising and exuberant response came from Latin America's other guardian of nationalism, Peronist Argentina. Argentine president Carlos Menem lavished praise on the new approach to strengthen U.S.-Latin American economic relations: "We consider this [the Enterprise Initiative] not as a proposal of a philan-thropic nature, based on a false paternalism. Nor does it grow out of strategic military considerations. On the contrary, it is an ambitious business proposition. Latin America is considered this time as a new entity, as a valid interlocutor able to talk in terms of mutual interests."[8]

An economic logic lurks beneath the movement toward hemi-spheric integration. In some ways, the 1990s resemble the 1930s, when the United States and Latin America turned to each other for bilateral trade agreements in the face of a world broken into exclusive trading blocs. The United States now finds it hard to penetrate Japan, and Latin America has had similar problems exporting to a self-absorbed Europe. As in the 1930s, the United States and Latin America have detected a commonality of economic interests, but unlike then, neither has an interest in withdrawing from the rest of the world. What the Western Hemisphere nations lack is a strategy of helping each other while at the same time prying open the GATT.

Just five years ago, the idea of a hemispheric option would have been inconceivable. Burdened by debt, brutalized by military dictators, defi-ant of or disgusted with U.S. policy, Latin America was no partner for the United States. Gradually, the old stereotypes are being replaced. A new image of modern, democratic technocrats is taking hold. Free, con-tested elections have been held in every country in Central and South

America, and all but Cuba in the Caribbean. There have been setbacks in Haiti, Peru, and Venezuela, while other countries like El Salvador, Guatemala, and Bolivia continue to struggle with the demons of their despotic past. But democracy is more widespread, if not deeper, than ever before, and the new democracies are on the frontier of devising collective mechanisms to defend each other from authoritarian reversals.

Most Latin American governments have laboriously but firmly reconstituted their macroeconomic bases. In all but Brazil, hyperinflation has been brought under control; debt service as a percent of gross product in all of Latin America declined from 64.3 in 1987 to 37.4 in 1991; capital is returning in large amounts; and the region's economy has begun to grow, by 2.8 percent in 1991, the first positive change since 1987. From 1986 to 1991, the U.S. has doubled both its exports to Latin America (to $63 billion, more than to Japan) and its foreign direct investment (to $72 billion).[9] Brazil is an exception to this rule, but when its huge engine is restarted, it will pull all of South America forward at an accelerating clip.

Even more startling than Latin America's turnaround has been the backward somersault of the United States. During the 1980s, as Latin America's debt began to decline, Washington's soared. Like our neighbors, we borrowed to consume, not to invest; the result is a decaying educational base, deteriorating infrastructure, declining productivity, and a widening gap between rich and poor. The only light amid the dismal economic performance is the growth of U.S. exports. Because our fastest-growing market is Latin America, and the Latin Americans' is the United States, the most practical reason for Washington to give the hemisphere a new priority is trade.

If NAFTA were expanded to include the Caribbean Basin and South America, the population covered by the new Western Hemisphere free trade area would nearly double—to 705 million people; the gross product would increase to nearly US$7 trillion; the region's exports would rise to US$620 billion. (See Table 6.1, pages 90–91.) In 1991, U.S. exports to both North and South America totaled US$145 billion, about 40 percent above the level of U.S. exports to the European Community. (See Table 6.4, page 98.) If South America were to reduce its barriers to U.S. goods, as Mexico has done in the last five years, one could anticipate a similar expansion in trade.

The prospect of integrating South America into NAFTA is somewhat comparable to the integration of Eastern with Western Europe. The purpose in both cases is to widen the market and better utilize the comparative

TABLE 6.4
U.S. EXPORTS TO NORTH & SOUTH AMERICA, EUROPE, AND ASIA (1945–1991)
(US$MILLIONS)

YEAR	NORTH & SOUTH AMERICA	EC	JAPAN & SOUTHEAST ASIA	WORLD
1945	2,438	3,114	1,381	10,527
1955	6,327	2,614	2,144	15,518
1965	10,196	5,252	5,180	28,461
1975	39,265	22,865	19,658	109,317
1980	79,076	58,855	44,512	225,722
1985	84,143	45,776	51,036	213,146
1986	86,449	53,222	52,981	227,159
1987	94,617	60,629	58,244	254,122
1988	115,334	75,864	88,841	322,426
1989	127,454	86,424	101,509	363,812
1990	137,082	98,129	109,054	393,592
1991	144,967	103,209	109,674	421,614

Sources: U.S. Department of Commerce, International Trade Administration, *U.S. Foreign Trade Highlights*, 1992, 1988, 1985; U.S. Department of Commerce, Office of Business Economics, *U.S. Exports & Imports 1923–1968*, November 1970; U.S. Department of Commerce, Bureau of Economic Analysis, *U.S. Merchandise Trade: Exports & Imports, 1965–1976*, 1977; U.S. Department of Commerce, Bureau of the Census, *Statistical Abstract of the United States*, various issues, 1950–1991.

advantages of the various countries within the free trade areas to forge more competitive industries. After the collapse of the Berlin Wall, many thought that Western Europe would have an easier time incorporating its Eastern neighbors than would North America integrating the Caribbean and Latin America, but several years later, it appears that the European challenge of introducing the market into state-controlled economies is far more difficult than Latin America's task of privatizing its state corporations and reducing its debt. In brief, the United States and the Western Hemisphere are better positioned to demonstrate to the world the way in which industrialized and developing countries can integrate their economies to mutual benefit.

After almost a decade of depression, Latin America in many ways is at the stage where Western Europe was following World War II. It has considerable unused industrial capacity, a highly trained labor force, and a proven capacity to grow. All it needs is capital (or reduced debt service) and a secure market for its exports. The sharp reduction of trade barriers in the Western Hemisphere could provide the stimulus for an economic takeoff.

When Salinas said that "we want Mexico to be part of the First World, not the Third,"[10] he was not only encouraging his countrymen to raise their hopes and standards. He was also implying that Mexico could exert greater influence in the international economic order if it aligned with the United States than if it remained oriented toward the developing world. This represents a momentous departure for Mexico and for all of Latin America. After having resisted the influence of United States for decades, the region has apparently concluded that its economic goals are more likely to be attained in cooperation with the North.

At the very end of the long NAFTA text—Chapter 22, Article 2205—sits a very brief and vague "accession clause":

> Any country or group of countries may accede to this Agreement subject to such terms and conditions as may be agreed between such country or countries and the Commission and following approval in accordance with the applicable procedures of each country.

It would appear that the negotiators either ran out of ideas, energy, or time because this so-called accession clause merely begs the question as to how to proceed with the expansion of NAFTA. Prior to his election as president of the United States, Bill Clinton endorsed the idea of extending the agreement in his address in North Carolina. "If we can make this agreement work with Canada and Mexico, then we can reach down into the other market-oriented economies of Central and South America to expand even further." President Bush had promised Chile that it would be next in line since its economy is the most open and ready to dock onto NAFTA.

There are several questions of procedure and direction to resolve: Should the United States wait several years for NAFTA to work before proceeding with other negotiations? Which country or countries should go first? Should special arrangements be made with the smaller, more vulnerable economies of Central America and the Caribbean? Should the new trade regime be opened to countries on other continents?

These are difficult questions, and while it would not be desirable to set down inflexible rules, a broader strategy would help to sort out the many demands that will be made on all the parties. Since the expansion of NAFTA will require, beyond consent from all three parties, an agreement on the specific terms of accession, these uncertainties will need to be answered within the Trade Commission before negotiations begin with other countries. It would be preferable to work the kinks out of NAFTA before it was extended. With regard to which country comes first, the three may want to encourage individual countries to reduce their trade and investment barriers to the level that Mexico achieved, but at the same time, perhaps some special allowance—a longer transition period, say—could be offered to the poorest countries in the Caribbean and Central America.

The Americas should not be an exclusive bloc, but it does not make much sense to open a hemispheric envelope to countries in Europe or Asia. It would be far better for Europe and Asia to demand commensurate changes in GATT. That would erode the edge off of NAFTA's privileges, but the whole world would benefit.

There are a number of reasons why regional agreements, such as NAFTA or an expanded Western Hemisphere free trade area, can promote more trade and help build a better GATT.

- NAFTA has developed formulas for dealing with issues like services that have eluded the grasp of the 105 nations negotiating under GATT. If a new approach, for example, NAFTA's dispute settlement procedure, works at the regional level, it can serve as a model for GATT.

- NAFTA could be a useful reminder to the European Community that if transatlantic trade talks sour, the United

States has other options. As the table on relative dependency showed, Japan and the nations of Europe would have more to lose than the United States from a round of market closings. This could lead Japan and Europe to take U.S. concerns about their trade policies more seriously. (The U.S. should only consider such tactics when a GATT panel has judged that its concerns are legitimate, as was the case in the agricultural dispute with the EC.) The EC's decision in November 1992 to finally try to solve the agricultural subsidies problem with the United States could be viewed as the first dividend of NAFTA.

- To the extent that NAFTA can help integrate a poor third world nation into a modern trade relationship, that could be an important model for the rest of the world, particularly at a moment when much of the developing world seems to be sliding toward marginalization.

- NAFTA promises to stimulate a substantial amount of new trade with few signs that it would lead to trade diversion. Increasing exports could be the primary engine for growth by the United States and the rest of the hemisphere in the coming years.

- NAFTA could help the three countries' industrial base become more efficient and competitive. The promise of the agreement could be an important incentive for Mexico and the rest of Latin America to consolidate their export-oriented economic policies and to reinforce their democracies.

NAFTA is not only an idea laden with hemispheric and global implications; it could also be a building block toward a better world trading system.

CHAPTER 7

CONCLUSIONS

There are no isolated problems; everything is part of everything else.[1]

—José López Portillo, 1977

When presidents present a difficult international issue to the American public, they are sometimes tempted to characterize the choice as between isolationism and internationalism. That is rarely the case. Even in the Senate discussion of whether the United States should join the League of Nations after World War I, the actual debate pitted the unilateral internationalism of Senator Henry Cabot Lodge and the cooperative internationalism of Woodrow Wilson. Today most U.S. leaders understand that, with an economy twice as dependent on world trade as it was two decades ago, the fate of the United States is tied to that of the world at large. The issue is not whether to pursue foreign policy goals or concentrate on domestic policy, but how to relate the two of them. NAFTA poses such a choice, and at just the right moment for the United States—the end of the cold war and the beginning of a new administration.

For NAFTA to succeed, it must join with a domestic policy that addresses the nation's social and economic problems. It also should be part of a new geostrategic vision. President Bill Clinton has stated that his top domestic objectives are not only to reactivate the U.S. economy but to modernize it, not only to save jobs but create better ones. To do so, he has pledged to improve the nation's infrastructure, provide better education and job training, enact investment tax credits, and stimulate research and development. These policies mesh neatly with the conditions that he has insisted must accompany the approval of NAFTA, and they will help the nation take advantage of NAFTA by sharing its benefits and mitigating its costs.

Because of technological innovations, a communications revolution, and the increased importance of trade, the pace of economic change in the world has accelerated. In such a world, management and capital move quickly, while labor remains stationary. The benefits of these changes have flowed disproportionately to those who are most mobile. In the absence of policies to help those who cannot adapt, society can become more unequal, as demonstrated by the United States in the 1980s. Redistributive mechanisms are essential to prevent the social fabric from tearing. There should be no pretense that equality of opportunity is sufficient; nor is it desirable to seek equality of results. The goal must be to limit inequalities. If the United States can define programs and redesign the tax systems to achieve a fairer balance, its new economic model could inspire the world. And if NAFTA truly incorporates social and environmental concerns, then trade policy will finally be rooted in a broader national consensus.

Next, the United States has to build durable partnerships with its neighbors in a North American Free Trade Area. Instead of reenacting scenes from a troubled history, both the United States and Mexico now have a stake in managing integration pragmatically. NAFTA offers Mexico its best opportunity to develop a modern economy, and no country will profit more from Mexico's development than the United States. That NAFTA was a Mexican initiative makes it easier for both sides to accept an agenda that will sometimes be uncomfortable for one or the other. Increasing and respectful contacts over the long term between the United States and Mexico, coupled with sustained economic growth, will provide a sound basis for a smooth and successful Mexican political transition to democracy.

In the post-cold-war world, the United States needs a new compass that realigns our geopolitical interests. Since World War II, we have sought allies to contain the Soviet Union; today, we need to seek markets and production-sharing ventures to compete against Germany, Japan, and the other industrialized nations. NAFTA and, before long, an extended Western Hemisphere free trade area offer the United

States those critical advantages. The agreement could become more than just a freer trade area, however; it could be the bond that reinforces a democratic ethos throughout the hemispheric community.

Vaclav Havel wrote about a paradoxical movement in the world "toward both integration and differentiation, toward both increasing the identity of the regions and diminishing the importance of frontiers."[2] The problem is how to relate sovereignty to integration, to unite the logic of politics with that of economics. By improving the standard of living of the peoples of Mexico and the United States and assuring the dignity of both peoples in a new cultural mosaic, NAFTA could bring an end to the mutually destructive, frustrating encounters of the past. But this will not be easy, and, in fact, NAFTA will probably create as many new sources of tension as it alleviates. Certainly, there will be sensitive political issues raised by the United States about the Mexican political system and about Mexican enforcement of workers' rights. A new style of approaching these issues is needed that will permit Mexico to complete its transition toward democracy without feeling as if it did so at the behest of its neighbor.

Issues will be tied together in new ways, but old national fears and instincts will always be present. In 1988, after a difficult Canadian election campaign in which the free trade agreement was the pivotal issue, Prime Minister Brian Mulroney said, "Americans might reflect on the fact that there is in Canada as in other industrialized countries a well of anti-Americanism. It happens that it's not enough to elect a dog-catcher, but this doesn't stop people from trying to whip it up."[3]

Canada is not unique in this. Each of the three countries is torn between a raw nationalism and a cooperative interdependence. An insensitive decision by the U.S. government could compel Mexicans to assert themselves in a defiant and unhelpful way, which would reinforce the defensiveness in the United States, and so on. The point is that a problem can originate anywhere, and historical sensitivities can compound the damage. Just as important, however, is that positive steps are also mutually reinforcing.

President Salinas has already responded positively to the Clinton proposals. He seems ready to move promptly to negotiate the side agreements in order to implement NAFTA.[4] In his state of the nation report on November 1, 1992, Salinas's principal theme was his determination to continue and consolidate his economic policies, of which NAFTA is a central element. Confidence in the country's economy could slacken if it takes too long to implement the agreement, and that could endanger efforts to bring about conditions for a free presidential election in 1994.

The congressional debate on NAFTA could be rough on Mexico. There will be few incentives for U.S. legislators to vote for it, and many of those who do might try to show their constitutents that they will not let Mexico take advantage of us. There was a similar political dynamic during the Senate vote on the Panama Canal Treaties in 1978, with senators voting in favor only after they extracted a pound of flesh from the Panamanian body politic. If this occurs, instead of focusing on what the United States could gain through NAFTA, attention could shift to what would be lost to Mexico. This issue should be discussed, but it is vital that policymakers keep two more important points in mind. First, both the United States and Mexico will benefit from freer trade and investment, but some groups within each nation will be hurt, so that policies are needed to share the benefits. Carlos Salinas made the second point when he noted that Americans are now losing jobs "to workers with very high wages in Germany and Japan, not to workers with low wages, like we have in Mexico."[5] Of course, U.S. jobs are lost in both directions, but his point is well taken.

To retain its competitive edge, the United States will have to continue to internationalize its economy. Its true economic competitors are not to the south or north but to the east and west—Japan and Germany. Mexico and Latin America are our natural partners in this new global economic competition.

Beyond NAFTA, the United States should seek a free trade community of democratic nations in the Americas. In addition to honing the competitive skills of the countries involved, the larger purpose is to forge a model of cooperation between industrialized and developing countries that will inspire other regions and narrow the gap that divides the prosperous from the indigent within countries and separates rich and poor nations.

With an infrastructure and a potential market roughly equivalent to Europe's at the beginning of the Marshall Plan, Latin America today offers the United States the key to enhancing its competitiveness, stimulating new growth, and invigorating its stalled leadership in the world. The first step toward this goal is to improve NAFTA and then ratify it.

CHRONOLOGY OF NORTH AMERICAN TRADE NEGOTIATIONS

1965   U.S.-Canadian Automotive Agreement.

1976–82   Presidency of José López Portillo of Mexico.

1980   Mexico decides not to join GATT.

1982   Debt crisis begins.

1982–88   Presidency of Miguel de la Madrid.

1984   Conservative government of Brian Mulroney elected in Canada. Government involvement in economy is reduced.

1986   U.S.-Canadian free trade negotiations begin. Mexico joins GATT. Uruguay Round of GATT trade negotiations begins.

1987   U.S.-Mexican "framework" agreement to consult on trade.

1988   Mulroney and President Reagan sign U.S.-Canadian Free Trade Agreement. Liberal and New Democratic parties of Canada oppose agreement, but Mulroney wins reelection with a plurality of 42 percent. Parliament then ratifies agreement. Easily ratified in the United States. Carlos Salinas de Gortari wins election in July in a controversial vote. His principal opponent, Cuauhtémoc Cárdenas, rejects the legitimacy of the outcome.

1989   Salinas liberalizes foreign investment rules and announces agreement with creditors to reduce Mexico's foreign debt.

1990   June 10: Presidents Bush and Salinas issue a joint statement endorsing the idea of a free trade agreement between the United States and Mexico. Their trade ministers begin work.

September 25: After recieving a formal request from Salinas for negotiations, Bush informs Congress of intent to negotiate a free trade agreement with Mexico. GATT negotiations fail to be completed in December as scheduled.

1991   February 5: Bush, Salinas, and Mulroney announce they will pursue trilateral negotiations to create a NAFTA.

March 1: Bush requests a two-year extension of fast-track authority.

May 1: In response to congressional concerns, Bush sends letter and Action Plan to Capitol Hill.

May 23–24: The House and Senate reject resolutions to disapprove the extension of fast-track procedures. Authority is extended for two years from March 3.

June 12: Trade officials from Mexico, Canada, and the United States officially begin negotiations.

August 18: Midterm elections in Mexico. PRI wins 320 seats in 500-seat Chamber of Deputies (61.4 percent of the vote), 31 of 32 Senate seats, and all six governorships at stake. After protests, PRI governors-elect in two states renounce their posts.

1992   February 25: The United States and Mexico sign Environmental Border Plan.

August 12: Negotiators reach agreement on NAFTA.

September 18: Bush notifies Congress of his intent to sign the final NAFTA agreement.

October 4: Democratic presidential candidate Bill Clinton gives speech on NAFTA in North Carolina.

October 7: Trade ministers of the United States, Mexico, and Canada initial the NAFTA agreement in San Antonio.

November 3: Clinton wins U.S. presidential election with a plurality of 43 percent.

November 5: Bush administration threatens to impose a 200 percent duty on French wine if Europeans do not end subsidies on some agricultural products.

November 20: The United States and Europe agree to cut farm subsidies, breathing life into long-stalled GATT negotiations.

December 17: Bush, Salinas, and Mulroney each sign NAFTA in their respective capitals.

1993   January 8: Meeting between President-elect Clinton and Salinas in Austin, Texas, where they confirm their intent to move promptly toward implementing the agreement.

January 20: Inauguration of Bill Clinton.

NOTES

I am indebted to John Bailey, Michelle Miller, Marion Creckmore, and Evelyn Huber for comments on an earlier draft, to Kjersten Walker for comments and research assistance, Steve Greenfield for copyediting, Michael Discenza for collecting the data and organizing the tables, and Felicia Agudelo for typing the tables and much else.

INTRODUCTION

1. Cited in Gary Langer, "What Voters Really Want From Clinton," *Wall Street Journal*, November 16,1992, p. A10.

2. John E. Reilly, ed., *American Public Opinion and U.S. Foreign Policy, 1991* (Chicago: Chicago Council on Foreign Relation, 1991), p. 27.

3. Data on 1990 and before are in Reilly, *American Public Opinion*, p. 27; and the 1987 survey, p. 25. The more recent staistics are from a CBS/*New York Times* poll in July 1992, cited by Ruy Teixeira and Guy Molyneux, *Economic Nationalism: An Emerging Issue for the 1990s* (Washington, D.C.: Economic Policy Institute, October 1992), pp. 14, 16.

4. Tim Golden, "Mexican President Seeks to Address Clinton's Concerns," *New York Times*, November 21, 1992, pp. A1,A2.

CHAPTER 1

1. Cited in Stuart Auerbach, "Five from Bush's Cabinet Laud Mexican Policies," *Washington Post*, August 9, 1987, p. A10.

2. Statements by Mexican President José López Portillo at a luncheon on February 14, 1979, for President Jimmy Carter, Mexico City, in *Public Papers of the Presidents, Jimmy Carter* (Washington, D.C.: Government Printing Office, 1979) vol. 1, p. 275.

3. Carlos Salinas de Gortari, *First State of the Nation Report*, November 1, 1989, published by the Embassy of Mexico in Washington, D.C., 1989, pp. 16–17.

4. Statement reprinted in *Foreign Broadcasting Information Service, Latin America* (FBIS), August 7, 1981, p. M1.

5. Testimony by Assistant Secretary of State for Inter-American Affairs Elliott Abrams before the U.S. Congress, Senate Committee on Foreign Relations, *Hearings: Situation in Mexico*, 99th Cong., 2d sess., May 13, 1986, p. 28.

6. Robert A. Pastor and Jorge G. Castañeda, *Limits to Friendship: The United States and Mexico* (New York: Alfred A. Knopf, 1988), p. 192.

7. Banco de México, *The Mexican Economy*, Mexico City, 1992, p. 206.

8. U.S. Department of Justice, Immigration and Naturalization Service, *Statistical Yearbook, 1990* (Washington, D.C.: Government Printing Office, December 1991), pp. 163, 180–82.

9. Cited in Robert A. Divine, *American Immigration Policy, 1924–1952* (New Haven: Yale University Press, 1957), p. 52.

10. "U.S. Shows Sharp Rise in Amount of Foreigners," *New York Times*, December 20, 1992, section 1, p. 14.

11. INS, *Statistical Yearbook, 1990*, p. 163.

12. Ibid., pp. 12, 48–50.

13. The characterization was by Felicity Barringer, "Census Shows Profound Change in Racial Makeup of the Nation," *New York Times*, March 11, 1991, pp. 1, 12. Also see U.S. Department of Commerce, Bureau of the Census, *1990 Census Profile: Race and Hispanic Origin*, no. 2, June 1991.

14. Joel Garreau describes one of nine "nations" in North America as extending north as far as Houston and Los Angeles and south as far as Monterrey. Joel Garreau, *The Nine Nations of North America* (New York: Avon Books, 1982).

15. Niles Hansen, *The Border Economy: Regional Development in the Southwest* (Austin: University of Texas Press, 1981), p. 155; F. Ray Marshall and Leon Bouvier, *Population Change and the Future of Texas* (Washington, D.C.: Population Reference Bureau, 1986), pp. 92–93.

16. William K. Stevens, "Census Report Finds a Return to Normal in Population Shifts," *New York Times*, October 1, 1987, pp. A1, A16; Carrie Teegardin, "Yankees Found the South to Their Liking in 1980s," *Atlanta Journal*, July 31, 1992, p. A8.

17. Study by Gary Orfield, cited by Amy Wallace, "U.S. Hispanics Fast Becoming a Class Apart," *Atlanta Journal*, September 30, 1987, p. A6.

18. U.S. Department of Commerce, International Trade Administration, *U.S. Exports to Mexico: A State-by-State Overview, 1987–90* (Washington, D.C.: Government Printing Office, August 1991), pp. 1–3. The statistics might exaggerate the degree to which trade originates in the two states

because some of the data is collected at the border and truck drivers might not know where the product originally came from.

19. For data from 1969 to 1983, see Joseph Grunwald and Kenneth Flamm, *The Global Factory: Foreign Assembly in International Trade* (Washington, D.C.: The Brookings Institution, 1985), Table 4–1, p. 140. For more recent data, see American Embassy, Mexico, *Foreign Investment Climate Report*, August 1991, p. 28; and Jeffrey J. Schott and Gary C. Hufbauer, *North American Free Trade: Issues and Recommendations*, (Washington, D.C.: Institute for International Economics, 1992), p. 96.

20. Keith Bradsher, "Trade Gap with Japan Is Widened," *New York Times*, November 19, 1992, p. C1.

21. Banco de México, *The Mexican Economy*, p. 260.

22. Ibid., p. 266.

23. INS, *Statistical Yearbook, 1990*, p. 166.

24. Rodolfo O. de la Garza et al., *Latino Voices* (Boulder, Colo.: Westview Press, 1992). For a summary of this study, see Roberto Suro, "Poll Finds Desire by Hispanic Americans to Assimilate," *New York Times*, December 15, 1992, pp. A1, A18.

25. American Embassy, Mexico, *Economic Trends Report*, May 1990, pp. 9–10.

26. Banco de México, *The Mexican Economy*, p. 15.

27. Ibid., p. 116.

28. For Mexican tariffs, see International Trade Commission, *Review of Trade and Investment Liberalization Measures by Mexico and Prospects for Future U.S.-Mexican Relations, Phase I: Recent Trade and Investment Reforms Undertaken by Mexico*, report no. 2275, April 1990, Tables 4-1, 4-2.

29. The 1986 figure is in Schott and Hufbauer, *North American Free Trade*, p. 73; the 1991 figure is from the American Embassy, Mexico, *Economic Trends Report*, February 1992, p. 2.

30. "Mexico Continues to Attract Foreign Investment," *El Financiero International* (Mexico City), June 1, 1992, p. 3.

31. Banco de México, *The Mexican Economy*, p. 142.

32. Salinas, *First State of the Nation Report*, pp. 8, 14.

33. Mark A. Uhlig, "Mining Laws Are Eased by Mexico," *New York Times*, September 28, 1990, p. D3.

34. Banco de México, *The Mexican Economy*, p. 213.

35. Mark A. Uhlig, "Mexico's Windfall Exceeds $3 Billion from Oil Price Rise," *New York Times*, February 12, 1991.

36. "The Latin Market Comes to Life," *The Economist*, June 8, 1991, pp. 79–80.

37. Larry Rohter, "North American Trade Bloc? Mexico Rejects Such an Idea," *New York Times*, November 24, 1988, pp. 25, 28. Salinas said, "I am not in favor of such a proposal. There is such a different economic level

between the United States and Mexico that I don't believe such a common market would provide an advantage to either country." He voiced similar comments in the fall of 1989.

38. Author's interview with President Carlos Salinas de Gortari, Mexico City, July 24, 1990.

39. Peter Truell, "Texans Use Their Influence with Bush to Open U.S.-Mexico Free-Trade Talks," *Wall Street Journal*, August 31, 1990, p. A12.

40. Robert D. Hershey, Jr., "Why Economists Fear the Deficit," *New York Times*, May 26, 1992, pp. C1, C3.

41. Sylvia Nasar, "The 1980s: A Very Good Time for the Very Rich," *New York Times*, March 5, 1992, pp. A1, C13.

42. Lynn A. Karoly, *The Trend in Inequality among Families, Individuals, and Workers in the United States: A Twenty-five Year Perspective* (Santa Monica, Calif.: RAND Corporation, 1992).

43. Lizette Álvarez cites a Gallup poll in March 1992, "Americans Tired of Welcoming Immigrants," *Miami Herald*, March 3, 1992, pp. A14, A15. Another poll by Roper in May 1992 found 86 percent describing "immigration" as a major issue, and 54 percent saying "too many immigrants are arriving each year." Cited in Julia Malone, "Too Many Immigrants?" *Atlanta Journal*, May 20, 1992, p. A3.

CHAPTER 2

1. If Congress wanted to amend the agreement, it could do so by passing a law mandating an alternative way of considering the legislation.

2. Author's interview with Cuauhtémoc Cárdenas, Mexico City, July 23, 1990.

3. Cuauhtémoc Cárdenas, "Misunderstanding Mexico," *Foreign Policy* 78 (Spring 1990): 115.

4. Carlos Salinas de Gortari, *First State of the Nation Report*, November 1, 1989, published by the Embassy of Mexico in Washington, D.C., 1989, p. 14.

5. Cited in Matt Moffett, "Mexico's Opposition Leader May Benefit if U.S. Congress Hinders Trade Accord," *Wall Street Journal*, April 26, 1991, p. 12.

6. On the question as to whether Mexicans had confidence in the registration list, 39 percent said no and 36 percent said yes. The poll was taken in August 1992, and published in *Este País*, December 1992, p. 39. On respect for the vote, see Miguel Basáñez, "Encuesta Electoral, 1991," *Este País*, August 1991, p. 6.

7. Tim Golden, "Mexicans Prepare Election Protests," *New York Times*, November 18, 1992, p. A4.

8. "Salinas Gives State of the Nation Address," reprinted in *Foreign Broadcast Information Service, Latin America* (FBIS), November 4, 1992, pp. 7–28.

9. Carlos Salinas de Gortari, *Second State of the Nation Report*, November 1, 1990, reprinted in *FBIS*, November 14, 1990, pp. 12–13. Cárdenas, "Misunderstanding Mexico," p. 117.

10. The polls are cited in a paper that argues for economic nationalism, "Economic Nationalism: An Emerging Issue for the 1990s," Ruy A. Teixeira and Guy Molyneux, Economic Policy Institute, Washington, D.C., October 1992, pp. 21–23.

11. Statement in the *Congressional Record*, October 30, 1991, p. S15524.

12. The Gallup organization was responsible for the surveys. They were published in the *Miami Herald*, June 3, 1992, p. 17.

13. Ronald Inglehart, Neil Nevitte, and Miguel Basáñez, "Convergence in North America: Closer Economic, Political, and Cultural Ties between the United States, Canada, and Mexico," unpublished manuscript, 1992.

14. Ibid., Chapter 1, p. 1.

15. See particularly Karl W. Deutsch et al., *Political Community and the North Atlantic Area* (Garden City, N.Y.: Doubleday, 1968).

16. Inglehart, Nevitte, and Basáñez, "Convergence in North America," Chapter 2, p. 15.

17. Ibid., Chapter 2, p. 12, Figure 2–3.

18. Ibid., Chapter 6, pp. 17–19.

19. John E. Reilly, ed., *American Public Opinion and U.S. Foreign Policy, 1991* (Chicago: Chicago Council on Foreign Relations, 1991), pp. 26–27.

20. Some question this assertion, but for a fuller development of the argument and of the political process described below, see Robert A. Pastor, "The Cry-and-Sigh Syndrome: Congress and U.S. Trade Policy," in Allen Schick, ed., *Making Economic Policy in Congress*, (Washington, D.C.: American Enterprise Institute for Public Policy, 1983), pp. 158–95.

21. Quoted in "Senate Completes Revision of Tariff after Weary Fight of Six Months, Eighteen Days," *New York Times*, March 23, 1930, pp. A1, A30.

22. For a review of U.S. trade policy, see Robert A. Pastor, *Congress and the Politics of U.S. Foreign Economic Policy* (Berkeley: University of California Press, 1980), Chapters 3–6.

CHAPTER 3

1. Cited in Peter Truell, "Administration Says Free Trade Pact with Mexico Will Create Jobs in U.S.," *Wall Street Journal*, April 12, 1991, p. A14.

2. "A Report to the President, the Congress, and the United States Trade Representative Concerning the North American Free Trade Agreement," submitted by the Advisory Committee for Trade Policy and Negotiations (ACTPN), September 1992, pp. 42–43.

3. "Statement by the President," White House Press Office, August 12, 1992.

4. *North American Free Trade Agreement*, report of the Labor Advisory Committee, AFL-CIO, Washington, D.C., October, 1992, p. 1.

5. The study is cited in Jim Kolbe, "Made in Mexico, Good for the USA," *New York Times*, December 13, 1987, section 4, p. 2.

6. The Stern Group for the U.S. Council of the Mexico-U.S. Business Committee, *Investment, Trade, and U.S. Gains in the NAFTA*, Washington, D.C., 1992, pp. 4, 37.

7. Rosemarie Philips, *U.S. Foreign Policy and Developing Countries* (Washington, D.C.: Overseas Development Council, 1991), Table 8, p. 33.

8. The U.S. International Trade Commission (ITC) held a symposium on February 24–25, 1992, and compiled twelve papers and twenty-four comments on different models. The result was published by the ITC, *Economy-Wide Modeling of the Economic Implications of a FTA with Mexico and a NAFTA with Canada and Mexico*, report on investigation no. 332-317, publication no. 2516, Washington, D.C., May 1992. A study by The Brookings Institution also includes several analyses based on models. See Nora Lustig, Barry P. Bosworth, and Robert Z. Lawrence, eds., *North American Free Trade: Assessing the Impact* (Washington, D.C.: The Brookings Institution, 1992).

9. Labor Advisory Committee, *North American Free Trade Agreement*, p. 1.

10. Congressional Research Service, Library of Congress, *North American Free Trade Agreement: Issues for Congress* (Washington, D.C.: Government Printing Office, July 12, 1991), p. 5.

11. U.S. exports increased from $12 billion to $33 billion, and the rule-of-thumb is that for each $1 billion of exports, 20,000 new jobs are created. See "Press Briefing by U.S. Trade Representative Carla Hills," White House, December 13, 1991.

12. ITC, *Economy-Wide Modeling of the Economic Implications of a FTA*, p. 14.

13. Ibid., p. 1.

14. Jeffrey J. Schott and Gary C. Hufbauer, *North American Free Trade: Issues and Recommendations* (Washington, D.C.: Institute for International Economics, 1992), pp. 52–61. For a comparison of the IIE model with several of the others, see pp. 58–59.

15. The 20,000 figure was used by the Commerce Department and U.S. Trade Representative Carla Hills (see her press conference at the White House, December 13, 1991). In their book, *North American Free Trade*, Schott and Hufbauer (see p. 55) use a figure based on U.S. Department of Commerce, *Statistical Abstract of the United States, 1990*, Table 1311, that suggests that 14,500 jobs are created per $1 billion of net improvement in the U.S. trade balance. That would translate into roughly 130,000 additional jobs. In July 1992, they revised that figure after the Commerce Department revised its multiplier to 19,600 jobs per $1 billion increase in exports. The result was a net growth of 171,000 jobs. Telephone conversation with Jeffrey Schott, November 24, 1992. For the job displacement figures, they cite Michael Podgursky, "The Industrial Structure of Job Displacement, 1979–1989," *Monthly Labor Review* (September, 1992): 17.

16. See Schott and Hufbauer, *North American Free Trade*, pp. 66–68.

17. U.S. Congress, Office of Technology Assessment, *U.S.-Mexico Trade: Pulling Together or Pulling Apart?* (Washington, D.C.: Government Printing Office, October 1992), p. 4.

18. Robert A. Pastor, ed., *Migration and Development in the Caribbean Basin* (Boulder, Colo.: Westview Press, 1985).

CHAPTER 4

1. "Precisa Salinas de Gortari el carácter del vínculo: Integración económica, no política, con EU," *La Jornada* (Mexico City), November 13, 1992, p. 1.

2. For a good discussion of these competing ideologies, see Michael Hart and Sushma Gera, "Trade and the Environment: Dialogue of the Deaf or Scope for Cooperation?" paper prepared for the Canada-U.S. Law Institute Conference on the Law and Economics of Environmental Regulation, Cleveland, April 24–26, 1992, pp. 1–10.

3. Special issue of *The Ecologist* 20, no. 6 (November/December 1990): 204.

4. For a good discussion of the various issues, see U.S. Congress, Office of Technology Assessment, *Trade and Environment: Conflicts and Opportunities* (Washington, D.C.: Government Printing Office, May 1992).

5. In response to President Bush's commitment to take environmental considerations into account, the National Wildlife Federation announced support of the fast-track authority; the Sierra Club and the Friends of the Earth opposed it; the National Audubon Society, the Environmental Defense Fund, and the Natural Resources Defense Council adopted a low profile on the issue.

6. "Mexico Delays Plans to Dam a Major River," *New York Times*, March 21, 1992.

7. See remarks by Stewart Hudson, National Wildlife Federation, "Opening Up the Debate: The Free Trade Agreement with Mexico and Environmental Concerns," at a Congressional Staff Briefing on the U.S.-Mexico Free Trade Agreement, Washington, D.C., January 15, 1991.

8. See, for example, *Crisis at Our Doorstep: Occupational and Environmental Health Implications for Mexico-U.S.-Canada Trade Negotiations*, National Safe Workplace Institute, Chicago, February 1991; and William Langewiesche, "The Border," *The Atlantic*, May and June 1992.

9. A report from the Texas Department of Health with technical assistance from the Centers for Disease Control, Atlanta, "An Investigation of a Cluster of Neural Tube Defects in Cameron County, Texas," July 1992.

10. See, for example, Judy Pasternak, "Firms Find a Haven from U.S. Environmental Rules," *Los Angeles Times*, November 19, 1991, reprinted in *Congressional Record*, November 22, 1991, p. E3967.

11. U.S. General Accounting Office, *U.S.-Mexico Trade: Some U.S. Wood Furniture Firms Relocated from Los Angeles Area to Mexico*, Report to the Chairman, Committee on Energy and Commerce, House of Representatives, GAO/NSIAD-91-191, April 1991, pp. 1–4. The wide range in the number of firms that might have relocated is attributable to the relatively small sample on which the projection was based.

12. See, for example, C. Fred Bergsten, Thomas Horst, and Theodore H. Moran, *American Multinational Corporations and American Interests* (Washington, D.C.: The Brookings Institution, 1978); Raymond Vernon, *Sovereignty at Bay: The Multinational Spread of U.S. Enterprises* (New York: Basic Books, 1971); and Richard J. Barnett and Ronald E. Muller, *Global Reach: The Power of the Multinational Corporation* (New York: Simon and Schuster, 1974).

13. Gene M. Grossman and Alan B. Krueger, "Environmental Impacts of a North American Free Trade Agreement," working paper no. 3914, National Bureau of Economic Research, Cambridge, Mass., 1991, p. 29.

14. Patrick Low, "Trade Measures and Environmental Quality: Implications for Mexico's Exports," paper presented at the Symposium on International Trade and the Environment, World Bank, Washington, D.C., November 21–22, 1991.

15. A study commissioned by the U.S. Trade Representative estimated that the border region would continue to grow at a rate of 5–15 percent without NAFTA, but the rate would be slower if it were approved. This study is cited by Jeffrey J. Schott and Gary C. Hufbauer, *North American Free Trade: Issues and Recommendations* (Washington, D.C.: Institute for International Economics, 1992), p. 138. Schott and Hufbauer concur that new firms are more likely to move deeper into Mexico with NAFTA.

16. Joseph Grunwald and Kenneth Flamm, *The Global Factory: Foreign Assembly in International Trade* (Washington, D.C.: The Brookings Institution, 1985), p. 161. A more recent estimate by the American Embassy in Mexico found average wages in the maquiladoras to be three times the Mexican minimum wage. American Embassy, Mexico, *Foreign Investment Climate Report*, August 1991, p. 28.

17. Grunwald and Flamm found that as the wage gap between the U.S. and Mexico widened, the problem of absenteeism and turnover of labor in the maquiladoras increased. *The Global Factory*, p. 179.

18. For a concise summary of the legislation and a discussion of its effects, see Schott and Hufbauer, *North American Free Trade*, pp. 134–53

19. Susan Fletcher and Mary Tiemann, "Environment and Trade," Congressional Research Service, Library of Congress, September 28, 1992, p. 9.

20. See Edward Cody, "Mexico Shuts Oil Refinery to Help Save Capital's Air," *Washington Post*, March 19, 1991, p. A22; Robert Reinhold, "Mexico Says It Won't Harbor U.S. Companies Fouling Air," *New York Times*, April 18, 1991, pp. A1, A10; "Mexico City Pollution Chief Defends Record," *El Financiero International* (Mexico City), May 4, 1992.

21. See Robert A. Pastor and Jorge G. Castañeda, *Limits to Friendship: The United States and Mexico* (New York: Alfred A. Knopf, 1988), Chapter 7.

22. For a detailed analysis of the 1983 plan, see Jan Gilbreath Rich, *Planning the Border's Future: The Mexican-U.S. Integrated Border Environmental Plan*, U.S.-Mexican Studies Program, Lyndon B. Johnson School of Public Affairs, University of Texas, Austin, March 1992, pp. 1–3.

23. "White House Fact Sheet: Review of Environmental Effects of Free Trade with Mexico," February 25, 1992.

24. Gilbreath Rich, *Planning the Border's Future*, pp. 26–46.

25. Grossman and Krueger, "Environmental Impacts of a North American Free Trade Agreement," p. 20. Mexico's per capita GDP in current value was $2,010, but it was near $5,000 in terms of purchasing power parity. Two other studies cited by Schott and Hufbauer, *North American Free Trade*, p. 131, note 2, arrived at similar conclusions.

26. Mancur Olson, Jr., *The Logic of Collective Action: Public Goods and the Theory of Groups* (Cambridge, Mass.: Harvard University Press, 1965) and *The Rise and Decline of Nations: Economic Growth, Stagflation, and Social Rigidities* (New Haven: Yale University Press, 1982).

27. The author is indebted to Stewart J. Hudson of the National Wildlife Federation for his analysis of NAFTA in a letter dated November 12, 1992, and in testimony he gave before Congress on September 16, 1992.

28. Cited in Keith Schneider, "Trade Pact vs. Environment: Clash at a House Hearing," *New York Times*, September 16, 1992, pp. C1, C14.

29. Jan Gilbreath Rich, "FTA Prompts Overhaul at Ecology Secretariat," *El Financiero International* (Mexico City), August 26, 1991, p. 13.

30. "Industry and Environment in Mexico," *Latin American Weekly Report*, October 1, 1992, p. 8.

31. Lawrence Kootnikoff, "Profits on Environment Has Business Seeing Green," *El Financiero International* (Mexico City), July 6, 1992, p. 14.

32. *Congressional Record*, May 24, 1991, p. S6799. On November 15, 1990, President Bush signed a Clean Air Act amendment that required significant cuts in the emissions of sulfur dioxide and nitrous oxide. An agreement between the United States and Canada that dealt with acid rain and other air quality issues went into force in March 1991. Schott and Hufbauer, *North American Free Trade*, p. 28.

33. The author is indebted to Dr. Howard Frumkin, director of the Division of Environmental and Occupational Health of Emory University's School of Public Health, Atlanta, for his ideas in this area. Dr. Frumkin heads a binational group that is looking into these issues.

34. For a devastating indictment of NAFTA's failure to address these issues, see *North American Free Trade Agreement*, report of the Labor Advisory Committee, AFL-CIO, Washington, D.C., October 1992, pp. 4–7.

35. See U.S. Department of Labor, Bureau of International Labor Affairs, *Labor Standards in Export Assembly Operations in Mexico and the Caribbean*

(Washington, D.C.: Government Printing Office, June 1990), p. 7; see also U.S. Department of Labor, Bureau of International Labor Affairs, *Worker Rights in Export Processing Zones: Mexico* (Washington, D.C.: Government Printing Office, August 1990), pp. 17, 67–68; Pastor and Castañeda, *Limits to Friendship*, p. 199.

36. International Labour Office, Geneva, *Yearbook of Labour Statistics, 1989–1990*, cited in Library of Congress, Congressional Research Service, *North American Free Trade Agreement: Issues for Congress*, March 25, 1991, p. 40.

37. Tom Barry, ed., *Mexico: A Country Guide* (Albuquerque, New Mexico: Inter-Hemispheric Resource Center, 1992), p. 183.

38. See "North American Labor Laws: How They Stack Up to Each Other," *El Financiero International* (Mexico City), May 25, 1992, pp. 14–15.

39. "Union Chief Approves Change to Labor Law," *El Financiero International* (Mexico City), June 29, 1992, p. 4.

40. Quoted by Talli Nauman, "Labor Laws Stand before Proposed NAFTA," *El Financiero International* (Mexico City), May 25, 1992, pp. 14–15.

41. See, for example, George E. Brown, Jr., J. William Goold, and John Cavanagh, "Making Trade Fair," *World Policy Journal* 8, no. 2 (Spring 1992): 309–27. Brown is a member of Congress and introduced H.R. 4883, April 9, 1992, calling upon U.S. negotiators to include "certain threshold protections regarding worker rights, agricultural standards, and environmental quality." The Charter was published by the Commission of the European Communities, Brussels, May 1990.

42. See Stephen A. Herzenberg, Jorge F. Pérez-López, and Stuart K. Tucker, "Labor Standards and Development in the Global Economy," a summary of a conference on the subject at the Overseas Development Council, Washington, D.C., December 1988.

43. Jerome I. Levinson, "The North American Free Trade Agreement: A Social Charter?" unpublished paper, 1992.

44. Barbara Crossette, "China Signs Pact with U.S. Meant to Curb Prison Labor on Exports," *New York Times*, August 8, 1992, p. 3.

45. U.S. Congress, House Foreign Affairs Committee, Subcommittee on Western Hemisphere Affairs, *Hearing: Update on Recent Developments in Mexico*, 102d Cong., 1st sess., October 16, 1991, pp. 2, 54–55.

46. "Tijuana's Midnight Express," *Newsweek*, November 23, 1992, p. 41.

47. "State Governor Apologizes for Supporting U.S. Aid Request," EFE News report, reprinted in *Foreign Broadcasting Information Service, Latin America*, December 10, 1978.

Chapter 5

1. George Stephanopoulos, Clinton's communications director, referred to Bush's program by saying "imitation is the sincerest form of flattery."

Cited in Richard L. Berke, "Bush Tells of Plan for More Spending to Train Workers," *New York Times*, August 25, 1992, pp. A1, A10.

2. *Economic Report of the President, 1992* (Washington, D.C.: Government Printing Office, February 1992), pp. 336, 404.

3. *North American Free Trade Agreement*, report of the Labor Advisory Committee, AFL-CIO, Washington, D.C., October 1992, pp. 5–7.

4. Jeffrey J. Schott and Gary C. Hufbauer, *North American Free Trade: Issues and Recommendations* (Washington, D.C.: Institute for International Economics, 1992), p. 60. Their estimates are high relative to the existing program, but probably low compared to what is needed. The Economic Dislocation and Worker Adjustment Assistance Act (EDWAA—Title III of the Job Training Partnership Act) provided benefits and retraining for 700,000 workers at an average cost of $1,700 per participant. Funding nearly doubled from $284 million at the beginning in July 1989 to $527 million in 1991.

5. Tim Golden, "Mexican President Seeks to Address Clinton's Concerns," *New York Times*, November 21, 1992 pp. A1, A2; Matt Moffett and Diana Solis, "Mexico Will Ask U.S., Canada for Aid to Smooth Its Entry to Free Trade Pact," *Wall Street Journal*, December 8, 1992, p. A11.

6. The author is indebted to Stewart J. Hudson of the National Wildlife Federation for these points.

7. U.S. Congress, Office of Technology Assessment, *U.S.-Mexico Trade: Pulling Together or Pulling Apart?* (Washington, D.C.: Government Printing Office, 1992), p. 38.

8. Dr. Howard Frumkin, director of the Division of Environmental and Occupational Health of Emory University's School of Public Health, Atlanta, educated the author on these issues and offered these ideas.

9. Joseph Kinney, executive director of the Mexico-U.S. Committee on Occupational and Environmental Health, expressed these ideas in a letter to the author dated November 12, 1992.

10. Luis Rubio, Director General of CIDAC (Centro de Investigación para el Desarrollo, A.C.), Mexico City, suggested several of these ideas.

11. Clyde H. Farnsworth, "U.S.-Canada Rifts Grow over Trade: Accusations on Beer, Cars, and Lumber," *New York Times*, February 18, 1992, pp. A1, C6.

12. Clyde H. Farnsworth, "U.S. Trade Pact a Spur to Canada," *New York Times*, July 22, 1992, pp. C1, C6.

13. See Michael Hart, "Dispute Settlement and the Canada-U.S. Free Trade Agreement," Occasional Paper in International Trade Law and Policy, The Norman Patterson School of International Affairs, Carleton University, Ottawa, Canada, August 21, 1990; Schott and Hufbauer, *North American Free Trade*, p. 38; Gary N. Horlick and F. Amanda DeBush, "Dispute Resolution Panels of the U.S.-Canada Free Trade Agreement: The First Two and One-half Years," unpublished paper, November 1, 1991.

14. Anthony Solomon, "Suggestions for Establishing a Special Bilateral Relationship," in Dwight S. Brothers and Adele E. Wick , eds., *Mexico's Search for a New Development Strategy* (Boulder, Colo.: Westview Press, 1990), p. 112.

15. Michael Hart, "After NAFTA: Trade Policy and Research Challenges for the 1990s," Occasional Paper, Centre for Trade Policy and Law, The Norman Patterson School of International Affairs, Carleton University, Ottawa, Canada, December 19, 1991, p. 9.

16. For a good discussion of the Mexican problem, see Talli Nauman, "The National Statistics Institute: How Far Can You Trust It?" *El Financiero International* (Mexico City), August 31, 1992, pp. 14–15.

17. Diana Solis, "Immigration Bill Would Expand Access to U.S.," *Wall Street Journal*, November 15, 1990, p. A20.

18. Rodolfo O. de la Garza et al., *Latino Voices* (Boulder, Colo., Westview Press, 1992). For a brief summary, see Roberto Suro, "Poll Finds Desire by Hispanic Americans to Assimilate," *New York Times*, December 15, 1992, pp. A1, A18. This public-opinion survey is consistent with others that have been taken in the past. See Robert A. Pastor and Jorge G. Castañeda, *Limits to Friendship: The United States and Mexico* (New York: Alfred A. Knopf, 1988), pp. 355–57.

19. For a detailed analysis of the issue of cultural assimilation and the extent to which the Mexican pattern is similar to others, see Pastor and Castañeda, *Limits to Friendship*, pp. 342–65.

20. Milt Freudenheim, "For Canada, Free Trade Accord Includes Higher Prices for Drugs," *New York Times*, November 16, 1992, p. A1; Philip J. Hilts, "Quality and Low Cost of Medical Care Lure Americans on Border to Mexico," *New York Times*, November 23, 1992, p. A8.

21. The author is indebted to Kjersten Walker for research assistance on European integration and its relevance to NAFTA.

22. Joseph A. McKinney, "Lessons from the Western European Experience for North American Economic Integration," paper prepared for a conference on Contemporary U.S.-Canada-Mexico Relations, University of Calgary, Calgary, Canada, May 2, 1991, p. 6.

23. Alan Riding, "Spain Aims for a Competitive Edge in a Unified Europe," *New York Times*, June 14, 1992, section 4, p. 11. On Spain's changes before entry, and the way in which it was "turning into the continent's Sun Belt," see Steven Greenhouse, "With Spain in Common Market, New Prosperity and Employment," *New York Times*, January 15, 1989, pp. A1, A9.

24. Donald J. Puchala, "The European Communities and the North American Free Trade Area," paper prepared for a conference on NAFTA at the Carter Center of Emory University, Atlanta, February 12, 1992, p. 3.

25. For an outline of this proposal, see Albert Fishlow, Sherman Robinson, and Raul Hinojosa-Ojeda, "Proposal for a North American Regional Development Bank," paper prepared for a conference sponsored

by the Federal Reserve Bank of Dallas, June 14, 1991. The author's refinements of the proposal benefited from a discussion of it at a meeting of experts sponsored by the Inter-American Dialogue and the Institute for International Economics in Washington, D.C., on June 23, 1992.

26. Moffett and Solis, "Mexico Will Ask U.S., Canada for Aid." Transcript of Clinton-Salinas Press Conference, Austin, Texas, January 8, 1993.

27. Banco de México, *The Mexican Economy*, Mexico City, 1992, pp. 156–59

28. *Latin American Weekly Report*, November 19, 1992, p. 7.

29. See George W. Schuyler, "Perspectives on Canada and Latin America: Changing Context . . . Changing Policy?" *Journal of Interamerican Studies and World Affairs* 33, no. 1 (Spring 1991).

CHAPTER 6

1. The analysis and arguments in this chapter are developed more fully in Robert A. Pastor, "The North American Free Trade Agreement: Hemispheric and Global Implications," paper prepared for the United Nations Economic Commission for Latin America and the Caribbean, to be published in spring 1993.

2. See, for example, Jagdish Bhagwati, "Jumpstarting GATT," *Foreign Policy* 83 (Summer 1991): 108.

3. "Milton Friedman Criticizes Regional Trade Agreements," *El Financiero International* (Mexico City), June 1, 1992, p. 3.

4. Lawrence B. Krause, "Regionalism in World Trade: The Limits of Economic Interdependence," *Harvard International Review* (Summer 1991): 4.

5. Ibid., p. 5.

6. Mark A. Uhlig, "Castro Gets Attention, but Not Money, from Latin Leaders," *New York Times*, July 21, 1991, p. A5.

7. Stuart Auerbach and Lewis H. Diuguid, "Bush Signs Three More Latin American Trade Pacts," *Washington Post*, June 28, 1991, p. A15.

8. Ibid.

9. U.S. Agency for International Development, *Latin America and the Caribbean: Selected Economic and Social Data* (Washington, D.C.: Government Printing Office, April 1992), pp. 3–5.

10. Carlos Salinas de Gortari, *Second State of the Nation Report*, November 1, 1990, reprinted in *Foreign Broadcast Information Service, Latin America*, November 14, 1990, p. 13.

CHAPTER 7

1. Cited in Viron P. Vaky, "Hemispheric Relations: Everything Is Part of Everything Else," *Foreign Affairs (1980)*: 59, no. 3, p. 616.

2. Vaclav Havel, "The Paradoxes of Help," *New York Times*, July 14, 1991, p. A19.

3. John F. Burns, "Mulroney to Push Approval of U.S.-Canadian Pact," *New York Times*, November 23, 1988, p. A6.

4. Tim Golden, "Mexican President Seeks to Address Clinton's Concerns," *New York Times*, November 21, 1992, pp. A1, A2.

5. Cited in Larry Smith, "Will His Plan Touch Our Lives?" *Parade*, August 9, 1992, p. 4.

INDEX

ABOUT THE AUTHOR

Robert Pastor has been Professor of Political Science at Emory University and Director of the Latin American and Caribbean Program at Emory's Carter Center since 1986. He was the Director of Latin American and Caribbean Affairs on the National Security Council from 1977–81. Dr. Pastor is the author of eight books, including *Whirlpool: U.S. Foreign Policy Toward Latin America and the Caribbean* (Princeton University Press, 1992); *Limits to Friendship: The United States and Mexico* (Alfred A. Knopf, 1988), with Jorge G. Castañeda; and *Condemned to Repetition: The United States and Nicaragua* (Princeton University Press, 1987). He also serves as Executive Secretary of the Council of Freely-Elected Heads of Government, a group of twenty-one Presidents of the Americas, chaired by former President Jimmy Carter. The Council has monitored and witnessed elections in Panama, Nicaragua, Haiti, Mexico, and Guyana.